From CALL to CLIENT:

The Criminal Defense Attorney's Complete Intake and Sales System

The Psychology-Based Method for Converting Clients Without Being Pushy

By Jay Ruane

DEDICATION

This book is dedicated to my own intake team and specialists over the years, including my current team, led by the intake master Daniel Martinez Arteaga, with his team of Jeronimo Maiquez, Sharon Aleman, Carlos Raveneau, and Brad Geltura. Your hard work for us helped me to refine this process and make our firm amazing at the intake process for criminal defense firms. Now we unleash it to the world of criminal defense attorneys!

TABLE OF CONTENTS

THE HIDDEN CRISIS IN CRIMINAL DEFENSE

Every month, thousands of people across the country reach out to criminal defense attorneys in their darkest hour. They've been arrested, charged, or are under investigation. They're scared, confused, and facing a legal system that seems designed to overwhelm them. These calls represent more than business opportunities—they're cries for help from people whose futures hang in the balance.

Yet here's the uncomfortable truth that most attorneys won't admit: the majority of criminal defense lawyers are terrible at intake and sales.

I don't say this to be harsh. I say it because I've lived it, studied it, and spent over twenty years developing solutions to fix it. When I started Ruane Attorneys in 2001, I was just another lawyer who went to law school to practice law, not to run a business. I thought good legal work would automatically translate into a successful practice. I was devastatingly wrong.

The reality hit me during my first few years of practice when I realized that many of the people who called me for help were ending up with cheaper, less qualified attorneys—or worse, trying to represent themselves. The difference wasn't my legal skills or even my prices in most cases. The difference was what happened in those crucial first few minutes when someone called my office in crisis.

That realization changed everything. It forced me to confront an uncomfortable question: If I couldn't effectively communicate my value and convert prospects into clients, how could I help anyone? More importantly, what happened to all those people who needed quality representation but ended up settling for less because I failed to effectively advocate for my own services?

This book exists because that problem is epidemic in our profession. Criminal defense attorneys across the country are losing potential clients not because they lack legal skills, but because they've never learned systematic approaches to intake and sales that work with people in psychological crisis.

Over the past two decades, I've built Ruane Attorneys from a solo practice into a multi-million-dollar criminal defense firm. More importantly, I've developed systematic approaches to intake and sales that work consistently across different personalities, experience levels, and market conditions. These aren't academic theories—they're battle-tested techniques refined through thousands of real-world applications.

WHY TRADITIONAL SALES TRAINING FAILS WITH CRIMINAL CLIENTS

The first thing you need to understand is that arrested people aren't normal consumers. They're not shopping for a car, comparing insurance policies, or choosing a restaurant. They're dealing with trauma, fear, shame, and overwhelming uncertainty about their future.

Traditional sales training assumes rational decision-making, price comparison shopping, and normal buyer psychology. None of these assumptions apply to someone who's been arrested. When someone calls you after being charged with DUI at 2 AM, they're not in a rational state of mind. They're in psychological crisis, and they need an entirely different approach.

This is why so many well-intentioned attorneys fail at intake. They treat scared, traumatized people like typical consumers, and the results are predictably poor. The prospect either shuts down, becomes defensive, or simply calls the next attorney on their list who might better understand their emotional state.

Everything you learned about sales in law school—which was probably nothing—or picked up from other industries can actually hurt you when dealing with criminal clients. The confident, assertive sales techniques that work in business-to-business sales will drive away people who are already feeling vulnerable and judged.

THE REAL COST OF POOR INTAKE SKILLS

Poor intake skills don't just cost you money—they result in worse outcomes for people who desperately need quality legal representation. When someone hires a cheaper, less qualified attorney because you couldn't effectively communicate your value, that's a failure of advocacy that starts with the intake call.

I've witnessed this tragedy countless times. A person facing serious charges calls multiple attorneys. The first few handle the call poorly—they're rushed, focused only on price, or fail to understand the client's emotional state. The prospect becomes frustrated and eventually hires whoever seems "good enough" at the right price point. Six months later, they're dealing with consequences that proper representation could have prevented.

Consider the real-world impact: Every person who calls you is dealing with one of the most stressful experiences of their life. They're facing prosecutors with unlimited resources, complex legal procedures they don't understand, and consequences that could affect them for years. Poor intake skills mean these people end up with inadequate representation at the moment they need skilled advocacy most.

This isn't just bad for individual clients—it's bad for the entire justice system. When quality attorneys can't effectively compete for clients because they lack intake skills, the market becomes dominated by firms that prioritize volume over excellence. The people who need the best representation end up with the loudest marketers instead of the most skilled advocates.

YOUR BUSINESS DEVELOPMENT PROBLEM

Most attorneys think they're bad at sales because they've never learned systematic approaches that work with criminal clients. This isn't about becoming a "salesperson"—it's about becoming an effective advocate for your own services so you can serve the clients who need your help.

When you master effective intake techniques, you'll see immediate improvements in multiple areas:

Conversion rates from initial calls to signed retainers will increase dramatically. Instead of converting one out of every five or six calls, you'll start converting two or three out of every five.

Average case values will rise because you'll attract better clients who understand and appreciate quality representation. When clients choose you based on value rather than price, they're willing to invest appropriately in their defense.

Client satisfaction will improve because clients feel confident in their choice from the very first interaction. When people hire you for the right reasons, they're more likely to be satisfied with the representation they receive.

Referral generation will multiply because satisfied clients become enthusiastic advocates for your practice. The clients who choose you based on trust and confidence are the ones who send their friends and family when they need legal help.

The attorneys who master intake and sales don't just make more money—they build practices that serve their communities better. When you can consistently convert quality prospects, you can be selective about the cases you take, invest in better support staff and technology, and focus on legal excellence instead of constantly worrying about revenue.

WHAT THIS BOOK WILL ACCOMPLISH

This book addresses the unique challenges of criminal defense intake by teaching you systematic approaches that work with people in crisis. Here's what you'll master:

Chapter 1 will teach you the psychology of the arrested client. You'll understand what's really happening in their minds when they call, the five emotional stages they go through, and why traditional sales approaches backfire completely. This psychological foundation is crucial because it affects every aspect of your interaction with prospects.

Chapter 2 introduces the B.U.I.L.D. Foundation—my systematic approach to every intake call that ensures consistency and effectiveness regardless of your personality or experience level. This framework has been refined through thousands of applications and works for introverted attorneys just as well as natural extroverts.

Chapter 3 focuses on mastering empathetic rapport building through specific language patterns and vocal techniques that create instant trust and connection with people in crisis. You'll learn exactly what to say, how to say it, and why it works psychologically.

Chapter 4 covers preselling your attorneys and firm—how to eliminate client anxiety about hiring attorneys they haven't met and create confidence in your legal team before they even speak with you. This is crucial for firms with multiple attorneys or when prospects need to make decisions quickly.

Chapter 5 addresses overcoming the Big Three Objections—the predictable objections that kill 80% of potential retainers and exactly how to address each one without being pushy or manipulative. These objections appear in virtually every practice area and market.

Chapter 6 teaches you the value proposition that converts—how to position your services so that price becomes secondary to the protection and peace of mind you provide. This isn't about being the cheapest option; it's about being the obviously best choice.

Chapter 7 covers closing without being pushy through consultative techniques that guide clients to hiring decisions while respecting their autonomy and decision-making process.

These techniques work because they align with how people in crisis actually make decisions.

Chapter 8 explains follow-up systems that work—how to stay connected with prospects who aren't ready to hire immediately and convert them when they are ready. Many potential clients need time to process their situation before making hiring decisions.

Chapter 9 reveals how to measure and improve your intake performance through data-driven analysis and AI-enhanced systems that transform subjective communication skills into objective, measurable data that drives consistent improvement.

Chapter 10 shows you how to build non-lawyer intake teams while maintaining legal compliance and conversion effectiveness. You'll learn what non-lawyers can and cannot do, why associates should never handle intake, and how to create compensation structures that align personal success with business success.

Chapter 11 provides the systematic approach to training your intake team that maintains quality while building capacity for practice growth. You'll learn how to hire for the right characteristics, implement structured onboarding, and maintain consistency across multiple team members.

Chapter 12 explores AI-powered intake optimization that represents the cutting edge of practice development. You'll discover how artificial intelligence can provide objective analysis of every conversation, enable real-time coaching, and create personalized follow-up content that dramatically improves conversion rates.

Chapter 13 covers stay top-of-mind follow-up systems that transform past clients into referral sources through value-first communication and helpful expert positioning that generates business for decades.

For firms ready to scale beyond individual attorney intake, we'll also cover advanced topics including measuring and improving your intake performance using data and analytics, training non-lawyer intake specialists while maintaining quality and legal compliance, building long-term client relationships that generate referrals for decades, and implementing systems that systematically improve conversion rates over time.

WHY THIS MATTERS TO YOUR PRACTICE AND THE JUSTICE SYSTEM

The skills you'll learn in this program serve multiple important purposes. On a practical level, they'll help you build a more successful and sustainable practice. But the impact goes far beyond business development.

Every person who calls you needs proper legal representation, but many will end up with inadequate counsel because quality attorneys can't effectively communicate their value. When you master these techniques, you're not just growing your practice—you're ensuring people get the representation they deserve during one of the most difficult periods of their lives.

Poor intake skills contribute to a justice system where the best marketing wins instead of the best legal representation. When skilled attorneys can't compete effectively for clients, the market rewards volume over quality. Your mastery of intake and sales helps restore the balance by ensuring that expertise and experience can compete effectively with aggressive marketing.

The ripple effects extend throughout your community. When you build a practice based on satisfied clients rather than aggressive marketing, you create a reputation that attracts both clients and referrals from other attorneys. This builds a sustainable practice that can focus on excellence rather than constantly chasing new business.

TRAINING APPROACH AND EXPECTATIONS

Everything I'm teaching you comes from real experience with thousands of intake calls over two decades. These aren't academic concepts borrowed from other industries—they're battle-tested techniques that work specifically with criminal clients.

You'll get proven systems, not theory. Each technique has been refined through practical application and measured results. You'll receive specific scripts and frameworks that you can implement immediately, but more importantly, you'll understand the psychology behind why these techniques work so you can adapt them to your personality and practice style.

Take notes, practice the techniques with colleagues, and apply what you learn to real situations. Question everything—these techniques should make sense logically and work practically in your specific market. Don't try to change everything at once; master one technique before moving to the next.

Most importantly, commit to excellence in serving your clients. The people who call you deserve the best representation possible, and that starts with ensuring they hire you instead of settling for less qualified counsel.

YOUR MISSION MOVING FORWARD

Over the following chapters, you're going to learn skills that most attorneys never master. You'll understand client psychology that even many experienced lawyers don't grasp. You'll develop systematic approaches that will make you exceptionally effective at converting prospects into clients.

But more importantly, you're going to learn how to ensure people get proper legal representation when they need it most.

The people who call you need your help. You need quality clients to serve. Your practice needs systematic growth to achieve its potential. And the justice system needs more attorneys who can effectively advocate for their services.

This book serves all of those goals simultaneously. Let's begin.

CHAPTER 1:

THE PSYCHOLOGY OF THE ARRESTED CLIENT

Sarah came to us with impeccable credentials. Five years of customer service experience at a luxury hotel chain, outstanding reviews from her previous employer, and an impressive track record of handling difficult situations with grace and professionalism. When we were looking for our first dedicated intake specialist, she seemed like the perfect fit.

I figured her experience dealing with upset hotel guests would translate perfectly to handling calls from potential clients. After all, how different could it be? People are people, right? Customer service is customer service.

I was about to learn an expensive lesson that would fundamentally change how we approach intake at our firm.

The call came in on a Tuesday afternoon. A first-time DUI case— a 34-year-old accountant who had been arrested the night before after leaving a client dinner. He was terrified, embarrassed, and completely out of his element. This should have been a straightforward conversion for us.

Sarah did exactly what her previous training had taught her to do. She opened by explaining our firm's credentials, talked about our win rate, mentioned the awards hanging on our office walls. Her presentation was professional, polished, and impressive. She covered all the bases that traditional customer service training says you should cover.

The prospect thanked her politely, said he'd "think about it," and hung up. Two hours later, we found out he had hired the attorney down the street—someone who charged half what we charge and had a fraction of our experience.

That single call probably cost us $5,000 in revenue. But more importantly, it cost that client the best representation he could have received during one of the most difficult periods of his life.

That's when I realized something that would reshape our entire approach to intake: an arrested client is not a normal customer. When someone calls a criminal defense attorney, they're not shopping for a car or comparing cell phone plans. They're in a genuine psychological crisis, and everything you think you know about traditional customer service not only doesn't apply—it can actually work against you.

THE FUNDAMENTAL DIFFERENCE

Understanding this difference is crucial for anyone involved in criminal defense intake. When most people think about customer service, they imagine rational consumers making logical decisions based on features, benefits, and price comparisons. They assume the customer has done research, knows what they want, and is simply looking for the best provider.

None of these assumptions apply to criminal clients.

When someone calls your office after being arrested, they're operating from a completely different psychological state. Their decision-making process has been hijacked by trauma, fear, and overwhelm. The logical, rational part of their brain—the prefrontal cortex that normally handles complex decisions—has essentially gone offline. The primitive, survival-oriented part of their brain has taken control.

This is why traditional sales techniques not only fail with criminal clients—they actively drive them away. When someone is already in a state of psychological crisis, pushy tactics don't create urgency, they create panic. Pressure doesn't motivate action, it triggers fight-or-flight responses that make people want to escape the conversation entirely.

THE TRAUMA RESPONSE

To understand how to effectively communicate with arrested clients, you first need to understand what arrest does to the human psyche. For most people, arrest is the most traumatic experience they've ever had. Even for minor charges, the process of being handcuffed, placed in a police car, processed through the booking system, and held in a cell creates immediate and profound psychological shock.

This trauma response manifests in several predictable ways that directly impact how prospects interact with attorneys:

Acute stress reaction affects their ability to process complex information. They may ask the same questions repeatedly, seem confused by straightforward explanations, or appear to not be listening when you're speaking. This isn't stubbornness or lack of intelligence—their brains literally cannot process detailed information while in crisis mode.

Shame and embarrassment make them reluctant to share details about their situation, even when those details are crucial for their defense. They're convinced that you'll judge them harshly once you know the "real" story, so they minimize, deflect, or omit important information.

Fear of judgment causes them to test you constantly to see if you'll treat them with respect or look down on them. They're hypersensitive to any hint of condescension, impatience, or moral superiority in your voice or words.

Overwhelming anxiety makes them susceptible to choosing the first option that seems to reduce their stress rather than the best option for their case. They're not necessarily looking for the most skilled attorney—they're looking for someone who can make them feel safe and protected right now.

THE FIVE EMOTIONAL STAGES

Through analyzing thousands of intake calls over two decades, I've identified five distinct emotional stages that arrested clients typically experience. These stages don't always occur in order, and prospects may cycle through them multiple times during a single conversation or through the lifespan of representation. However, recognizing which stage someone is in allows you to tailor your approach for maximum effectiveness.

Stage 1: Shock and Denial

"This can't be happening to me." "There must be some mistake." "I wasn't even that drunk." "The officer seemed really nice—surely this is just a misunderstanding."

Prospects in this stage are psychologically protecting themselves by minimizing the situation. They often focus on procedural mistakes, question the validity of the charges, or insist that everything will be dismissed quickly once the "real facts" come out.

Your response needs to acknowledge their feelings while gently introducing reality. Avoid the temptation to immediately correct their misunderstandings about the law or their situation. Instead, focus on validating their emotional state while positioning yourself as someone who can help them navigate whatever comes next.

What works: "I understand this is shocking and unexpected. Many of my clients feel exactly the same way when they first call. Let's talk about what actually happened and what your options are moving forward."

What doesn't work: "Actually, the officer doesn't need to be correct about everything for you to be convicted." This may be legally accurate, but it pushes them deeper into denial and resistance.

Stage 2: Anger and Blame

"The cops were wrong." "They violated my rights." "This is all BS—I want to fight this." "I should sue them for false arrest."

In this stage, prospects are pushing back against the reality of their situation. They're angry at the police, angry at the system, and sometimes even angry at you for not immediately telling them the case will be dismissed. They want to fight, to prove their innocence, to make someone pay for the injustice they've suffered.

The key here is not to argue with them or try to immediately correct their misconceptions. Let them vent. Acknowledge their frustration. Then redirect them toward productive next steps. Fighting their anger will only push them away and confirm their suspicion that you're part of the system that's working against them.

What works: "I can hear how frustrated you are, and I don't blame you. This system can feel really unfair, especially when you're experiencing it for the first time. Let's talk about how we can channel that energy into building the strongest possible defense."

What doesn't work: "Well, actually, the officer had every right to stop you because..." This immediately puts you on the side of law enforcement in their mind, destroying any chance of building rapport.

Stage 3: Bargaining and Minimization

"Maybe I don't really need a lawyer." "Can't I just represent myself?" "It's just a first offense—how bad could it be?" "My buddy says public defenders are just as good as private attorneys."

This is often the most dangerous stage for conversion because prospects start minimizing the seriousness of their charges and convincing themselves they can handle the situation with minimal help or expense. They're looking for reasons to avoid the cost and complexity of hiring a private attorney.

You need to educate without lecturing. Help them understand the real stakes—not just potential jail time, but employment implications, professional licensing issues, future consequences they haven't considered. But do this through questions and gentle guidance rather than fear-based pressure tactics.

What works: "I understand wanting to handle this yourself—it shows you're the kind of person who takes responsibility. Can I ask what you do for work? Because sometimes there are professional implications that people don't realize until it's too late."

What doesn't work: "You're crazy if you think you can handle this yourself. Do you have any idea how serious these charges are?" This approach triggers defensive responses and makes them more likely to dig in on self-representation.

Stage 4: Depression and Catastrophizing

"My life is ruined." "Everyone's going to find out." "I'll never get another job." "My family is going to disown me."

In this stage, prospects swing from minimizing their situation to catastrophizing it. They're convinced their career is over, their reputation is destroyed, and their life as they know it is finished. They feel hopeless and overwhelmed by the magnitude of what they're facing.

This is actually a favorable stage for conversion because they clearly recognize they need help, but you need to provide hope alongside expertise. Show them you've helped people in similar situations get their lives back on track. Share success stories (without violating confidentiality) that demonstrate positive outcomes are possible.

What works: "I know this feels overwhelming right now, and those feelings are completely normal. I've helped hundreds of people who felt exactly like you do, and most of them look back on this as just a difficult period they got through, not something that defined their entire life."

What doesn't work: "Don't worry about it—everything will be fine." This minimizes their legitimate concerns and makes you sound naive about the real consequences they might face.

Stage 5: Acceptance and Readiness

"I need professional help." "I want to hire the best attorney I can afford." "What do I need to do to get started?"

This is your ideal prospect—they understand they need an attorney and they're ready to make a decision. But don't get overconfident here. They still need to trust that you're the right attorney for them, and they may be calling multiple lawyers to compare options.

Focus on demonstrating competence and building confidence in your ability to handle their specific situation. Be prepared to discuss next steps, timeline, and what they can expect from the process.

What works: "I'm glad you're taking this seriously and looking for proper representation. Let me tell you exactly how we'd handle a case like yours and what you can expect each step of the way."

What doesn't work: Launching into a aggressive sales pitch because you sense they're ready to buy. Even prospects in the acceptance stage can be scared away by pushy tactics.

WHY TRADITIONAL SALES TECHNIQUES BACKFIRE

Understanding these emotional stages explains why conventional sales approaches fail so spectacularly with criminal clients. Traditional sales training assumes rational decision-making, price comparison shopping, and normal buyer psychology. It teaches you to establish credibility through credentials, create urgency through scarcity, and close through persistence.

Every one of these approaches can trigger defensive responses in people who are in psychological crisis.

The Credential Trap

Most attorneys open intake calls by establishing their credentials: years of experience, number of cases handled, bar admissions, awards won. The logic seems sound—establish credibility early to build confidence in your abilities.

But to a scared client, this often feels like intimidation rather than reassurance. They're already feeling small and powerless. When you lead with your impressive background, you're inadvertently emphasizing the power differential between you. They may interpret this as arrogance or as evidence that you're too important to really care about their "small" case.

The Fee Discussion Mistake

Traditional sales training suggests discussing price early to qualify prospects and avoid wasting time on people who can't afford your services. This approach assumes rational consumers who want to understand their options and make informed financial decisions.

Criminal clients aren't rational consumers. They're drowning in legal stress, and when you immediately add financial stress to their burden, you often trigger a shutdown response. They become focused on finding the cheapest option rather than the best representation, or they become paralyzed by the financial implications and postpone hiring anyone.

The Pressure Problem

Traditional closing techniques rely on creating urgency and pushing for immediate decisions. "You need to decide right now." "This offer won't be available tomorrow." "Other people are interested in this same opportunity."

People in crisis don't respond well to pressure—they respond to safety and support. When you push for immediate decisions, you trigger their fight-or-flight response. They may agree to hire you just to end the conversation, but they're likely to experience buyer's remorse and potentially fire you before the representation begins.

The Comparison Confusion

Standard sales approaches often involve comparing your services to competitors, highlighting your advantages and their disadvantages. This assumes customers who want to make informed comparisons and choose the best option.

Criminal clients are already overwhelmed and confused. When you add more information to compare and evaluate, you're increasing their cognitive load during a period when their decision-making capacity is already compromised. They need simplification, not additional complexity.

THE TRUST-BUILDING IMPERATIVE

If traditional sales techniques don't work with criminal clients, what does? The answer lies in understanding that trust trumps logic with people in crisis. Every time.

Your primary objective in the first few minutes of any intake call isn't to sell your services—it's to create what I call psychological safety. You want prospects to feel like they called the right place, that they're going to be protected rather than judged, and that you understand what they're going through.

The Seven-Second Window

Research shows that people form first impressions within seven seconds of meeting someone. But with criminal clients, I've learned something even more important: first impressions during crisis situations tend to be permanent.

If you mishandle those first seven seconds—if you come across as pushy, arrogant, or money-focused—you'll rarely recover. But if you create immediate psychological safety, if you demonstrate understanding and competence without being overwhelming, they'll often become your most loyal clients.

Voice tone carries more weight than words during these crucial first moments. I've analyzed thousands of intake calls, and I can predict conversion rates with remarkable accuracy just by listening to the first thirty seconds. It's not what you say—it's how you say it.

Calm, confident, and caring beats polished and professional every time when dealing with people in crisis.

Building Credibility Through Understanding

Here's the counterintuitive part that most attorneys miss: you build more credibility by demonstrating understanding than by listing accomplishments. When you say, "I understand how scary this must be for you," you're showing expertise in what matters most to them right now—their emotional state.

You demonstrate knowledge through strategic questions rather than through bragging. Instead of saying, "I've handled 2,000 DUI cases," you ask, "Were you coming from dinner when this happened?" That question tells them you understand typical DUI scenarios without making the conversation about your experience.

You position yourself not as a vendor selling services, but as an advocate and protector who understands their world. This distinction is crucial because it aligns with what they're actually looking for—someone who can guide them through an unfamiliar and frightening process.

PRACTICAL APPLICATION

Let me show you how understanding client psychology translates into actual conversation techniques. Here are two approaches to the same scenario—a first-time DUI client calling for help:

Traditional Approach:

"Good morning, this is Attorney Johnson. I've been practicing criminal defense for fifteen years and have handled over 2,000 DUI cases with a 95% success rate. I'm board certified in criminal law and have been named to Super Lawyers for the past five years. Our standard fee for DUI representation is $5,000, and we'll need a retainer before we can get started. When would you like to schedule a consultation?"

Psychology-Based Approach:

"Hi, this is Sarah from the Johnson Law Firm. I'm here to help you. Can you tell me a little bit about what happened?... Oh my goodness, are you okay? That sounds really frightening... I want you to know you called the right place. We handle situations just like this every day, and we're going to take good care of you. Let's talk about what happens next and how we can help you get through this."

The difference is striking. The traditional approach triggers every psychological defense mechanism we've discussed. It emphasizes the power differential, adds financial stress, and pressures for immediate decisions. The psychology-based approach creates safety, demonstrates understanding, and positions the attorney as a protector rather than a vendor.

Why the Psychology-Based Approach Works

In the second example, you're acknowledging their emotional state before addressing any practical concerns. You're creating psychological safety before trying to establish credibility or discuss business details. You're positioning yourself as someone who cares about them as a person, not just as a potential source of revenue.

The traditional approach makes the conversation about you and your accomplishments. The psychology-based approach makes it about them and their needs. This distinction is fundamental to effective criminal defense intake.

IMPLEMENTING PSYCHOLOGICAL AWARENESS

Understanding client psychology is the foundation of effective intake, but knowledge alone isn't enough. You need to develop the ability to quickly assess where prospects are emotionally and adjust your approach accordingly.

Listen for emotional indicators in their voice and word choice. Are they speaking quickly (anxiety)? Slowly (depression)? Are they using minimizing language (denial) or catastrophic language (overwhelm)? Are they asking lots of questions about the process (acceptance) or focused on proving their innocence (anger)?

Match their emotional energy appropriately. If they're panicked, you need to be calmer than they are. If they're depressed, you need to provide hope without being unrealistically optimistic. If they're angry, you need to acknowledge their frustration without getting drawn into their emotional state.

Focus on creating connection before providing information. People in crisis need to feel understood before they can process logical information effectively. Spend time acknowledging their emotional state and validating their concerns before moving into practical discussions about legal strategy or fees.

CHAPTER SUMMARY

The psychology of arrested clients is fundamentally different from normal consumer psychology. People who have been arrested are in genuine crisis, operating from survival mode rather than rational decision-making mode. Traditional sales techniques that work in other contexts not only fail with criminal clients—they actively drive them away by triggering defensive responses.

Successful criminal defense intake requires understanding the five emotional stages that arrested clients experience: shock and denial, anger and blame, bargaining and minimization, depression and catastrophizing, and acceptance and readiness.

Your approach must be tailored to whichever stage the prospect is experiencing during your conversation.

Trust building is more important than credibility establishment with people in crisis. Your primary goal in the first few minutes of any intake call should be creating psychological safety rather than selling your services. When prospects feel understood and protected, they become much more receptive to information about how you can help them.

The key insight that transforms intake effectiveness is this: make the conversation about them and their needs, not about you and your accomplishments. Demonstrate understanding through strategic questions and empathetic responses rather than through credentials and case statistics.

In the next chapter, we'll build on this psychological foundation by introducing the B.U.I.L.D. system - my systematic approach that ensures consistent, effective intake regardless of your personality type or experience level. You'll learn the specific steps and language patterns that create trust and guide prospects toward hiring decisions that serve their best interests.

CHAPTER 2:

THE B.U.I.L.D. FOUNDATION - YOUR SYSTEMATIC APPROACH

Understanding client psychology is only half the battle. You can know everything about why arrested clients behave the way they do, but if you don't have a systematic approach to apply that knowledge, you're still going to wing it on every call. And winging it means inconsistent results.

I learned this lesson the hard way during our firm's early growth phase. We had attorneys and staff members who could have brilliant intake calls one day and completely blow easy conversions the next. Their success depended entirely on their mood, energy level, and whether they happened to connect naturally with a particular caller.

This inconsistency was killing us. We were losing potential clients not because we lacked skill, but because we lacked system. Some days our conversion rates would be excellent. Other days they'd be terrible. There was no predictability, no way to train new staff effectively, and no way to identify what was working versus what was failing.

That's when I developed the B.U.I.L.D. system—a proven, step-by-step methodology that my team now uses on every single intake call. This isn't theory. This is the exact framework that helped us build a multi-million-dollar criminal defense practice with conversion rates that consistently exceed industry standards.

Here's my promise to you: this framework works consistently every time, regardless of your experience level, regardless of your personality type, and regardless of the type of case. When you have a system, you don't have to be brilliant on every call. You just have to be systematic.

THE B.U.I.L.D. METHODOLOGY OVERVIEW

B.U.I.L.D. stands for:
- Breathe & Build Rapport
- Understand the Situation
- Identify Specific Concerns
- Listen Actively
- Develop Trust & Demonstrate Value

Each component builds on the previous one, creating a natural flow that guides prospects from initial contact to hiring decision. The system works because it aligns with how people in crisis actually process information and make decisions, rather than how we think they should make decisions.

More importantly, the B.U.I.L.D. system is designed to be repeatable. Once you master it, you can train others to use it effectively. It creates consistency across your entire intake process, regardless of who's handling the calls.

B - BREATHE & BUILD RAPPORT

The "B" in B.U.I.L.D. starts before you even answer the phone. Most attorneys think rapport building begins when you start talking. That's wrong. It starts with your mental and physical preparation.

Personal Preparation Before Answering

Your mental state directly affects your voice tone, which prospects pick up on within seconds. If you just finished a frustrating conversation with a prosecutor, or you're stressed about another case, that energy will come through in your voice. Arrested clients are hypersensitive to emotional cues, and they'll interpret stress or distraction as lack of care or competence.

Mental State Check and Energy Assessment

Take thirty seconds before answering any intake call to assess your mental state. Are you calm and focused, or are you carrying stress from previous conversations? Are you genuinely ready to help someone in crisis, or are you going through the motions?

If you're not in the right headspace, take a moment to reset. This isn't about being perfect—it's about being present and authentic when someone needs your help most.

Environment Setup

Eliminate noise and distractions completely. I don't care how good you think you are at multitasking—your potential client will hear you typing, shuffling papers, or dealing with interruptions. They're already feeling vulnerable and uncertain. Don't make them compete for your attention.

Close your email. Turn away from your computer screen. Put down whatever you're working on. This call could represent thousands of dollars in revenue and, more importantly, it represents someone's future. Give it the attention it deserves.

Breathing Technique for Calm Confidence

Here's what I teach my team: three deep breaths before answering any intake call. In through the nose for four counts, hold for four, out through the mouth for six. This activates your parasympathetic nervous system and creates the calm confidence that builds trust.

This isn't new-age nonsense—it's basic physiology. When you control your breathing, you control your nervous system, which controls your voice tone, which affects how prospects perceive you. Calm confidence is contagious, especially with people who are anxious and scared.

Immediate Rapport Building Techniques

When you answer that phone, you have seconds to create connection. Everything you do in those first moments either builds trust or creates distance.

Matching and Mirroring Speaking Pace

If they're speaking slowly because they're processing trauma, don't hit them with rapid-fire questions. If they're speaking quickly because they're anxious, don't respond with a monotone drone. Mirror their emotional energy while maintaining your own calm confidence.

This isn't about manipulation—it's about meeting people where they are emotionally. When someone feels like you're on the same wavelength, they're more likely to trust you with their fears and concerns.

Active Listening Signals

Use phrases that clients can hear over the phone to know you're truly listening: "I understand," "That sounds really difficult," "Help me understand that better." These aren't just pleasantries—they're psychological safety signals that encourage continued sharing.

Most people have never had a lawyer actually listen to them before. When you demonstrate genuine interest in their perspective, you immediately differentiate yourself from every other attorney they might call.

Empathy Statements

Have authentic empathy statements ready, but don't use them mechanically. "I'm so sorry you're going through this" isn't just being nice—it's strategic trust building in a moment of crisis. But it has to be genuine. People in crisis can detect insincerity immediately.

The key is to acknowledge their emotional state before trying to address their practical concerns. Emotions must be validated before logic can be processed.

U - UNDERSTAND THE SITUATION

This is where most attorneys go wrong. They think "understanding the situation" means getting the facts of the case. That's backward thinking. The facts are in the police report. What you need to understand is their world right now—their fears, their concerns, their priorities.

Information Gathering Without Interrogation

Your job isn't to conduct a legal interview during the intake call—it's to understand their perspective and concerns. Use open-ended questions that feel conversational, not clinical.

Instead of "What were you charged with?" try "Help me understand what happened from your perspective." The first question feels like an interrogation. The second feels like an invitation to share their story.

Understanding Charges vs. Understanding Concerns

The charges are legal facts that you can research and analyze later. Their concerns are emotional realities that drive their decision-making process right now. Someone might be charged with a minor offense but terrified about losing their job. Someone else might be facing serious charges but primarily worried about telling their spouse what happened.

Focus on understanding what matters most to them, not what you think should matter most based on the legal severity of their charges.

Identifying Urgency Markers

Look for urgency markers beyond just court dates. Are there employment deadlines? Professional licensing renewals? Immigration concerns? Family court proceedings? Security clearance reviews? These create emotional urgency that moves people to action faster than abstract legal timelines.

When you identify multiple urgency markers, you can prioritize them based on what matters most to the client, not just what happens first chronologically.

Strategic Question Framework

I give my team three go-to questions that work in virtually every situation:

"Help me understand what happened from your perspective..."

This invites them to tell their story in their own words. You're not asking for legal facts—you're asking for their experience. This question often reveals details that wouldn't come up in a standard legal interview, and it shows that you value their perspective.

"What are you most concerned about right now?"

This cuts through everything else to identify their primary fear or worry. The answer might surprise you. Someone facing a DUI might be most concerned about a child custody hearing next month. Someone charged with assault might be most worried about their security clearance review.

"What questions do you have that I can help answer?"

This positions you as a resource and helper rather than an interrogator. It also gives you insight into what they've already researched or what other attorneys might have told them. Most importantly, it demonstrates that you want to provide value even before they hire you.

Notice the psychology here: you're not interrogating them, you're inviting them to share. You're positioning yourself as someone who wants to help, not judge.

I - IDENTIFY SPECIFIC CONCERNS

This is where we go deeper than the surface. Most clients won't tell you their real concerns upfront—either because they're embarrassed, or because they don't even realize what they should be worried about.

Going Deeper Than Surface Issues

Employment and Professional Licensing Concerns

Will they lose their job? Can they travel for work? Will this affect their security clearance? Are there professional licensing implications they haven't considered? Many clients focus on criminal penalties while missing the professional consequences that might have longer-lasting impact.

Family Impact and Relationship Consequences

How do they tell their spouse? What about custody issues if they're divorced? What will their parents think? Are there immigration implications for family members? These concerns often create more anxiety than the legal penalties themselves.

Financial Worries Beyond Legal Fees

Will they lose income if they can't travel for work? Are there insurance implications they haven't considered? What about that mortgage application they have pending? These secondary financial impacts often dwarf the cost of legal representation.

Timeline Pressures and Deadline Stress

When do they have to tell their employer? When does their professional license come up for renewal? When is their next custody hearing? These deadlines create urgency that goes beyond court dates and can be powerful motivators for immediate action.

The Iceberg Principle in Client Psychology

What clients say first is just the tip of the iceberg. Their surface concerns mask deeper fears that actually drive their decision-making:

Surface concern: "How much does this cost?"
Deeper concern: "Will I lose my job over this?"
Real concern: "How do I tell my family what happened?"

Your job is to identify the real concern, because that's what you're actually solving for them. Price objections are rarely about price—they're about underlying fears that affordable legal help might not address their real problems.

When you understand the iceberg principle, you can address objections before they arise by speaking to the deeper concerns rather than just the surface issues.

L - LISTEN ACTIVELY

Active listening is more than just staying quiet while they talk. It's a skill that requires practice and intentionality, especially when dealing with people in crisis who may struggle to articulate their concerns clearly.

Advanced Techniques Beyond Just Hearing Words

Reflective Listening and Emotional Validation

When they say "I'm worried about losing my job," you respond with "It sounds like your job security is a major concern for you right now." You're reflecting back not just the words, but the emotion behind them.

This technique serves two purposes: it confirms that you understand their concern correctly, and it validates their emotional response. Many people worry that their fears are irrational or overblown. When you reflect their concerns back to them, you're confirming that their worries are legitimate and understandable.

Strategic Silence for Processing

After they finish explaining something difficult, don't immediately jump in with your response. Let there be two or three seconds of silence. This gives them permission to go deeper, to share what they might have held back initially.

Most people are uncomfortable with silence and will fill it with additional information, often revealing concerns or details they wouldn't have shared otherwise. Strategic silence is one of the most powerful tools in your intake arsenal.

Common Active Listening Mistakes to Avoid

Interrupting with Immediate Solutions

They're not ready for solutions yet—they need to feel heard first. When you jump straight to problem-solving, you're skipping the trust-building phase that makes clients receptive to your advice.

Jumping Directly to Legal Analysis

Save the legal strategy discussion for after you've built trust and understood their priorities. Leading with legal analysis makes you sound like every other attorney they might call.

Multitasking During Intake Calls

This call determines whether you get a substantial retainer or lose a potential client forever. Give it your full attention. Clients can hear typing, paper shuffling, and distracted responses. These signals tell them they're not your priority.

Focusing on Your Next Question Instead of Their Current Answer

If you're thinking about what to ask next, you're not really listening to what they're saying now. Authentic listening requires being present in the moment, not planning your next move.

D - DEVELOP TRUST & DEMONSTRATE VALUE

This is where everything comes together. Trust isn't built through bragging about your accomplishments—it's built through authentic actions and strategic value demonstration that shows you understand their world.

Trust Building Through Authentic Actions

Admitting Limitations and Knowledge Gaps Honestly

If you don't know something, say so. "That's a great question, let me find out the specific answer for you." Clients trust attorneys who are honest about what they don't know more than attorneys who pretend to know everything.

This counterintuitive approach builds credibility because it demonstrates integrity and competence. When you're honest about small knowledge gaps, clients trust that you're being honest about everything else.

Setting Realistic Expectations from the First Conversation

Don't oversell the outcome to close the deal. Give them a realistic range of possibilities and explain the factors that will influence the result. Clients who hire you based on realistic expectations are more satisfied with your representation and more likely to refer others.

Following Through on Small Promises Immediately

If you say you'll email them something, do it before the end of the day. If you promise to call them back at a specific time, call them back on time. Small follow-throughs build confidence in big follow-throughs.

These micro-commitments are low-risk ways to demonstrate reliability. When you consistently follow through on small promises, clients trust that you'll follow through on the big ones that matter for their case.

Value Demonstration Without Bragging

Use Anonymized Case Examples with Similar Situations

"I had another client last month with a very similar situation, and here's how we approached it..." This shows experience without making the conversation about your accomplishments. It also helps them visualize positive outcomes for their own situation.

Make sure your examples are truly similar and that you maintain client confidentiality. The goal is to provide hope and demonstrate competence, not to violate ethical obligations.

Process Explanation That Shows Thoroughness

Walk them through your systematic approach: "Here's how we handle cases like yours. First, we do a complete case analysis to identify every possible defense. Then we investigate the facts to find weaknesses in the state's case. Finally, we develop a personal strategy to minimize the impact on your job and family."

This demonstrates that you're not just going to show up and hope for the best. You have a systematic approach that addresses their legal concerns and their personal priorities.

Resource Sharing That Demonstrates Expertise

"I'm going to send you a guide I wrote about what to expect in Connecticut DUI cases." This shows you're an expert without having to tell them you're an expert. It also provides immediate value that differentiates you from other attorneys they might be considering.

Make sure any resources you share are genuinely helpful and well-written. Poor-quality materials will hurt your credibility rather than help it.

PUTTING B.U.I.L.D. INTO PRACTICE

Let me walk you through how this sounds in a real call:

[Phone rings - three deep breaths before answering]

B - Build Rapport: "Hi, this is Sarah from Ruane Attorneys. I understand you're calling about a legal matter. I'm here to help you. How are you doing today?" *[Wait for response, match their energy level]*

U - Understand: "Help me understand what happened from your perspective..." *[Let them tell their story]* "That sounds really scary. What are you most concerned about right now?"

I - Identify: "You mentioned being worried about your job—tell me more about that. Are there any professional licenses involved? Any upcoming reviews or applications you're concerned about?"

L - Listen: *[Reflective listening]* "So if I'm understanding correctly, your biggest worry isn't just the legal consequences, but how this might affect your career and your family's financial security. Is that right?"

D - Develop: "I want you to know that we handle cases like this regularly, and we understand how to protect not just your legal interests, but your professional interests too. Let me tell you about our three-layer approach..."

Common Implementation Mistakes and Corrections

Don't Rush Through the Steps

Each letter in B.U.I.L.D. should feel natural and conversational, not like you're checking boxes on a list. The framework provides structure, but your personality and genuine concern should still come through.

Don't Skip Steps Because You Think You Know What They Need

Every client is different, even if their charges look similar. Someone facing their second DUI might be more concerned about their professional reputation than someone facing their first. Take time to understand each person's unique situation.

Don't Make It Sound Scripted

Use the framework as structure, not as a script. Your responses should be authentic and tailored to the specific conversation you're having. The system provides guardrails, not dialogue.

Don't Ignore Emotional Cues

If someone becomes emotional during the call, address it immediately. "I can hear how upset you are about this. Take your time." Don't push forward with your agenda when they need emotional support.

MEASURING B.U.I.L.D. EFFECTIVENESS

The B.U.I.L.D. system is designed to be measurable and improvable. Track these metrics to ensure you're implementing it effectively:

Conversion Rate Improvement

Your overall conversion rate should improve within the first month of consistent B.U.I.L.D. implementation. Track conversions by day of the week, time of day, and type of case to identify patterns.

Call Duration and Depth

Effective B.U.I.L.D. calls are usually longer than rushed sales calls but result in higher conversion rates. You should see an increase in average call length accompanied by better conversion rates.

Client Satisfaction and Retention

Clients who hire you through effective B.U.I.L.D. conversations are typically more satisfied with your representation because they hired you for the right reasons. They're also more likely to refer others and less likely to fire you during representation.

Follow-Up Conversion Rates

Not every prospect will hire you immediately, but effective B.U.I.L.D. conversations create stronger relationships that convert over time. Track how many prospects who don't hire immediately eventually become clients.

CHAPTER SUMMARY

The B.U.I.L.D. system provides a systematic approach to intake that works consistently regardless of your personality type, experience level, or the specific type of case. By following this framework, you can eliminate the inconsistency that kills conversion rates and build a predictable, scalable intake process.

Breathe & Build Rapport starts before you answer the phone and focuses on creating psychological safety through preparation and authentic connection.

Understand the Situation goes beyond gathering legal facts to understand the client's perspective, concerns, and priorities.

Identify Specific Concerns digs deeper than surface issues to uncover the real fears and worries that drive decision-making.

Listen Actively uses advanced techniques like reflective listening and strategic silence to make clients feel truly heard and understood.

Develop Trust & Demonstrate Value builds credibility through authentic actions and strategic value demonstration rather than bragging about accomplishments.

When you implement B.U.I.L.D. consistently, you create a systematic approach that serves both your business development goals and your clients' needs for competent, caring representation during their time of crisis.

In the next chapter, we'll dive deep into mastering empathetic rapport building techniques. You'll learn the specific language patterns and psychological triggers that create instant trust, even with the most skeptical or defensive clients. These techniques build on the B.U.I.L.D. foundation to create even stronger connections with prospects who need your help.

CHAPTER 3:

MASTERING EMPATHETIC RAPPORT BUILDING

There's a critical difference between sympathy and empathy in legal intake, and getting this wrong will kill your conversion rates faster than any other mistake you can make.

Sympathy is saying "I'm sorry that happened to you." It's acknowledging someone's pain from the outside, offering condolences for their situation. Empathy is saying "That sounds incredibly overwhelming—help me understand how this is affecting your daily life." It's stepping into their experience and demonstrating that you understand not just what happened, but what it means to them.

Here's the brutal truth that most attorneys don't want to acknowledge: rapport determines conversion rates more than price, experience, or legal expertise. I've watched attorneys with half my experience and twice my fees consistently out-convert seasoned lawyers simply because they mastered empathetic connection with prospects in crisis.

You can have the best legal arguments in the world, the most impressive track record, and the most reasonable fees in your market. But if your potential client doesn't trust you, doesn't feel understood by you, doesn't believe you actually care about their outcome—they're going to hire someone else. Usually someone who charges less and offers inferior representation.

This isn't speculation. I've analyzed thousands of intake calls over two decades, and the pattern is unmistakable. The attorneys who create genuine empathetic connection convert prospects at rates that seem impossible to those who rely primarily on credentials and logic.

The encouraging news is that empathetic rapport building isn't a personality trait you're born with or without. These are specific, learnable techniques that any attorney can master, regardless of their natural communication style or level of extroversion.

THE SCIENCE OF INSTANT CONNECTION

Understanding the neuroscience behind rapport building gives you a significant advantage in intake conversations. When you know how human brains naturally create connection, you can consciously activate these processes to build trust faster and more reliably.

Mirror Neurons and Natural Matching

Your brain contains specialized cells called mirror neurons that automatically synchronize with the person you're talking to. These neurons fire both when you perform an action and when you observe someone else performing the same action. They're responsible for our ability to feel empathy, understand emotions, and connect with others on a neurological level.

During intake calls, you can consciously activate this mirroring process to build faster rapport, but you need to be strategic about how you do it.

Speaking Pace Synchronization Without Mimicking

If they're talking slowly because they're processing trauma, don't hit them with rapid-fire questions. Their slow pace indicates they need time to process information and emotions. When you match their deliberate pace, you're signaling that you respect their processing time and won't rush them through important decisions.

Conversely, if they're speaking quickly because they're anxious, don't respond with a monotone drone. Their rapid speech indicates urgency and emotional intensity. When you match their energy level while maintaining calm confidence, you show that you understand the importance of their situation.

The key is matching their energy without mimicking their exact speech patterns, which feels artificial and manipulative. You want to create harmony, not imitation.

Energy Level Matching for Emotional Comfort

If someone calls you at an 8 out of 10 anxiety level, and you respond at a 3 out of 10 energy level, there's an immediate psychological disconnect. They feel like you don't understand the urgency or importance of their situation. You're not taking their crisis seriously.

You don't need to match their panic or overwhelm—that would be counterproductive. But you do need to match their sense of urgency and importance. When they feel like you "get it," they become much more receptive to your guidance and advice.

Breathing Pattern Awareness and Unconscious Connection

Here's something most people don't realize: when you consciously slow down your breathing during difficult calls, it actually helps calm the other person. They unconsciously synchronize their breathing patterns to yours, which triggers their parasympathetic nervous system and reduces their stress response.

This isn't metaphysical—it's basic human physiology. When you model calm, controlled breathing, you're literally helping to regulate their nervous system through unconscious mirroring.

Emotional Contagion in Phone Conversations

Emotional contagion is the phenomenon where emotions spread from person to person through unconscious mimicry and synchronization. In face-to-face interactions, this happens through facial expressions, body language, and vocal cues. On the phone, vocal cues become even more important because they're the primary way emotions are transmitted.

Managing Your Own Emotional State

Your emotional state directly affects client comfort and decision-making ability. If you're stressed, rushed, or distracted, they will feel it immediately through your voice tone, pacing, and word choice. If you're calm, confident, and focused, they'll feel that too.

Before every intake call, implement what I call an "emotional reset": three deep breaths, shake out any physical tension, and remind yourself that your job is to help this person feel safe and supported. This isn't about manufacturing fake emotions—it's about accessing your genuine desire to help people in crisis.

Projecting Calm Confidence

Calm confidence isn't about being unrealistically positive or promising outcomes you can't guarantee. It's about genuine confidence that you've helped people in similar situations before and you can help them too. It's confidence in your systematic approach to difficult cases, even when outcomes are uncertain.

This type of confidence is reassuring to people in crisis because it suggests competence without arrogance, experience without jadedness, and professionalism without coldness.

LANGUAGE PATTERNS THAT BUILD TRUST

The specific words and phrases you use during intake calls either create psychological safety or trigger defensive responses. After analyzing thousands of conversations, I've identified language patterns that consistently build trust with criminal clients.

Validation Phrase Categories

Emotional Validation Phrases:
- "That sounds incredibly stressful and overwhelming."
- "I can completely understand why you're worried about that."
- "Most people in your situation feel exactly the same way."
- "Your concerns make perfect sense given what you're facing."

Notice the psychology here: you're not minimizing their experience or offering false reassurance. You're validating that their emotional response is appropriate and understandable. This is crucial because many people worry that their fears are irrational or overblown.

Situational Validation Phrases:
- "This is definitely not something you should have to handle alone."

- "You're smart to be thinking about these implications."
- "These are exactly the right questions to be asking."
- "It makes sense that you'd want to understand all your options."

These phrases validate their decision-making process and intelligence, which helps counteract the shame and self-doubt that often accompany criminal charges.

Normalization Phrases That Reduce Shame

Criminal clients often feel like they're the only person who's ever been in their situation. They're embarrassed, ashamed, and convinced that everyone will judge them harshly. Your job is to normalize their experience without minimizing its importance.

Effective Normalization Phrases:
- "This type of situation is actually quite common."
- "You're definitely not the first person to ask that question."
- "Many of our clients have similar concerns and priorities."
- "This is something we handle regularly and know how to address."

These phrases reduce isolation and shame while maintaining the seriousness of their situation. You're not saying their case isn't important—you're saying they're not alone in facing these challenges.

Partnership Phrases That Build Alliance

This is where you shift from being a vendor they're evaluating to being an advocate who's already on their team. Partnership language creates collaboration rather than salesmanship.

Effective Partnership Phrases:
- "Let's figure this out together step by step."

- "I'm here to help guide you through this process."
- "We'll handle this systematically so nothing gets missed."
- "You don't have to navigate this alone anymore."

Notice how these phrases position you as being on the same side, working toward the same goals. This alliance mentality is crucial for building the trust necessary for high-stakes legal representation.

Words and Phrases to Completely Avoid

Certain words and phrases destroy rapport instantly with criminal clients. Avoid these at all costs:

"I understand" - Unless you've personally been arrested for similar charges, you don't understand their exact experience. Use "I can imagine how difficult this must be" instead.

"Don't worry about it" - This is dismissive of legitimate concerns and makes you sound naive about real consequences. Use "Let's address that concern directly" instead.

"You should have..." - This is judgmental and shame-inducing when they're already vulnerable. Focus on moving forward rather than past decisions.

"Typically" or "Usually" - These words create uncertainty about their specific case. Be more specific: "In cases like yours, we often see..."

VOICE TONE AND PACING MASTERY

Research shows that communication is 55% body language, 38% tone of voice, and only 7% actual words. On the phone, you lose the body language component, which means your tone of voice becomes even more critical for building rapport and conveying competence.

The Modified Communication Formula for Phone Intake

When you can't rely on body language, your voice tone carries the entire emotional weight of the conversation. Here's how to optimize each component:

Physical Positioning Affects Voice Quality

Even though they can't see you, your posture directly affects your voice quality. Sit up straight, smile while talking, and use hand gestures even though they're not visible. These physical behaviors change your vocal tone in ways that prospects can hear and feel.

Tone of Voice Becomes Your Primary Rapport Tool

Your voice tone must convey calm confidence, genuine concern, and professional competence simultaneously. This requires conscious practice and awareness.

Words Become More Precisely Important

Since you can't rely on facial expressions or body language to clarify meaning, your word choice becomes critically important. Every phrase must be carefully chosen to create the emotional response you want.

Specific Tone Techniques

Lowering Pitch to Convey Authority and Calm

When you're nervous or rushed, your voice naturally gets higher in pitch. Higher-pitched voices are perceived as less authoritative and more anxious. Consciously lower your pitch to project confidence and calm competence.

Slowing Pace for Important Information

When you're explaining something critical—legal consequences, next steps, or important deadlines—slow down your speaking pace by about 20%. Give their brain time to process complex information while demonstrating that you consider this information important enough to emphasize.

Strategic Pauses for Emphasis and Processing

After they tell you something emotional or significant, pause for 2-3 seconds before responding. This shows that you're actually absorbing what they said rather than just waiting for your turn to talk. Strategic silence also encourages them to share additional information they might have held back.

Volume Control for Creating Intimacy

Lower your volume slightly when discussing sensitive topics like family impact, job concerns, or personal consequences. This creates psychological intimacy and makes them feel like you're having a private, confidential conversation rather than a business transaction.

Advanced Pacing Strategies

Start Faster to Match Initial Anxiety

Meet them where they are emotionally when they first call. If they're speaking quickly due to anxiety, start at a similar pace to create initial connection.

Gradually Slow Down to Calm Their State

As the conversation progresses, gradually slow your pace to guide them to a calmer emotional state. This technique helps them move from crisis mode to decision-making mode.

Speed Up for Action Items

When discussing next steps, solutions, or positive actions, increase your pace slightly to create momentum and urgency around moving forward.

Pause Before Important Information

"Here's what we're going to do..." [pause] "Here's how we can help..." [pause]. These strategic pauses make them lean in mentally and signal that important information is coming.

AVOIDING THE "SALES PERSON" TRAP

The fastest way to kill rapport with criminal clients is to sound like you're selling them something. Criminal clients are already skeptical of attorneys and the legal system. If you come across as sales-focused rather than help-focused, you've lost them immediately.

Consultant vs. Vendor Positioning

Lead with Strategic Questions, Not Feature Statements

Instead of opening with "We have 20 years of experience handling cases like yours," start with "Help me understand your biggest concern about this situation." The first approach makes it about you and your credentials. The second makes it about them and their needs.

Focus Entirely on Their Needs First

Make the first half of the call about understanding their world, not explaining your world. They don't care about your experience until they trust that you understand their specific situation and concerns.

Be Genuinely Willing to Refer Out

"If this isn't something we can help you with effectively, I'll make sure you get connected with someone who can." This statement builds massive trust because it demonstrates that you prioritize their needs over your revenue.

Create Collaboration, Not Persuasion

You're not trying to convince them to hire you. You're trying to solve their problem together and determine if you're the right person to help them do that.

Professional vs. Friendly Balance

Striking the right balance between professional competence and human warmth is crucial for effective rapport building.

Warm and Approachable but Competent and Authoritative

You want them to feel comfortable talking to you, but also confident in your ability to handle their case effectively.

Warmth without competence feels unprofessional. Competence without warmth feels cold and intimidating.

Accessible and Understanding but Not Overly Familiar

Show genuine concern and understanding without crossing professional boundaries. You're not becoming their therapist or their friend—you're their potential attorney who genuinely cares about their wellbeing.

Caring and Concerned while Maintaining Boundaries

Demonstrate genuine concern about their situation and its impact on their life without getting emotionally enmeshed in their crisis. You can care deeply about their outcome while maintaining the professional distance necessary for effective representation.

PRACTICAL EXAMPLES AND APPLICATIONS

Let me show you how these principles translate into actual conversations with different types of callers:

The Angry/Hostile Caller

Rapport-Destroying Approach: "Sir, you need to calm down and listen to what I'm telling you."

Rapport-Building Approach: "I can hear how frustrated you are about this situation, and that frustration makes complete sense given what you've been through. Let's channel that energy into figuring out the best way forward for you."

The first response triggers defensiveness and escalates conflict. The second validates their emotion while redirecting it toward productive action.

The Scared First-Time Offender

Rapport-Destroying Approach: "Don't worry about it—we'll take care of everything. This happens all the time."

Rapport-Building Approach: "I can imagine how scary this must be—this is probably your first time dealing with anything like this. Many of our clients feel exactly the same way when they first call. Let's walk through this step by step so you understand what's happening and what your options are."

The first response minimizes legitimate fears and creates unrealistic expectations. The second validates their fear while providing hope and structure.

The Repeat Offender

Rapport-Destroying Approach: "What did you get arrested for this time?"

Rapport-Building Approach: "Help me understand what's going on. I know this isn't easy to deal with again, and I'm sure you have concerns about how this might be different from last time. What are your main priorities right now?"

The first response is judgmental and assumes the worst. The second acknowledges their experience while focusing on their current concerns.

The Family Member Calling

Rapport-Destroying Approach: "He needs to call me himself. I can't discuss his case with you."

Rapport-Building Approach: "I understand you're concerned about your son, and I can hear how much this is stressing your family. While I'll need to speak with him directly about his case, let me help you understand what options might be available and how we can best support him through this."

The first response is technically correct but dismissive and unhelpful. The second acknowledges their concern while explaining boundaries and offering appropriate assistance.

Complete Conversation Comparison

Rapport-Destroying Approach:
"Ruane Law Firm, this is Jennifer. How can I help you today? Okay, what were you charged with? When's your court date? Have you been arrested before? Our fees start at $3,500 for DUI cases. Do you want to schedule a consultation?"

Rapport-Building Approach:
"Hi, this is Jennifer from Ruane Attorneys. I understand you're calling about a legal matter, and I'm here to help you. How are you holding up today? [Listen to response] That sounds really overwhelming, and I can hear how worried you are. Help me understand what happened so I can figure out the best way to help you..."

The difference is striking. The first approach treats them like a case to be processed. The second treats them like a person in crisis who needs support and guidance.

MEASURING RAPPORT EFFECTIVENESS

Effective rapport building creates measurable changes in prospect behavior during intake calls:

Longer Call Duration with Higher Engagement

When prospects feel understood and comfortable, they share more information and ask more questions. Effective rapport building typically increases call duration while also improving conversion rates.

More Personal Information Shared

Prospects who trust you will share concerns about family, employment, and personal consequences that they wouldn't share with attorneys who fail to build rapport.

Questions About Your Process and Experience

When prospects trust you, they start asking about how you handle cases, what they can expect, and what makes your approach different. They're evaluating you as a solution rather than shopping for prices.

Reduced Price Objections

Prospects who feel understood and confident in your abilities are less likely to make price the primary decision factor. They ask about value and outcomes rather than just costs.

CHAPTER SUMMARY

Empathetic rapport building is the foundation of effective criminal defense intake. It requires understanding the neuroscience of human connection, using specific language patterns that build trust, mastering voice tone and pacing techniques, and avoiding the sales approaches that destroy trust with people in crisis.

The key insights for mastering empathetic rapport building are:

Empathy beats sympathy because it demonstrates understanding rather than just acknowledgment of someone's pain.

Your emotional state directly influences client comfort through emotional contagion, making your personal preparation before calls crucial.

Specific language patterns create psychological safety through validation, normalization, and partnership phrases that make prospects feel understood and supported.

Voice tone and pacing become even more critical on phone calls where visual cues are absent, requiring conscious control of pitch, pace, volume, and strategic silence.

Consultant positioning beats vendor positioning because it creates collaboration rather than sales pressure, which is essential for building trust with skeptical, traumatized prospects.

When you master these techniques, you'll find that prospects become more open, more trusting, and more likely to hire you based on confidence rather than price. More importantly, you'll be providing genuine support to people in crisis while building the kind of practice that attracts clients who value quality representation.

In the next chapter, we'll address the specific challenge of preselling your attorneys and firm. You'll learn how to build confidence in your legal team and capabilities before prospects have met anyone else at your firm, which is crucial for converting calls into consultations and consultations into retainers.

CHAPTER 4:

PRESELLING YOUR ATTORNEYS AND FIRM

One of the biggest challenges in criminal defense intake is a reality that most firms don't adequately address: clients often hire your firm and get assigned to an attorney they've never spoken to. This creates massive anxiety that can derail even the best intake conversations.

Think about it from the client's perspective. They just had one of the most traumatic experiences of their life. They've called multiple attorneys, trying to figure out who can help them. They finally decide to hire your firm based on a conversation with an intake specialist, but now they're being told they'll work with someone they've never met.

Immediately, their minds start racing with questions: "Who is this person? Do they know what they're doing? Will they care about my case? Are they experienced enough? Am I making the right decision? Should I have hired that other attorney instead?"

Your job is to eliminate that anxiety completely before they even sign the retainer agreement. When you presell effectively, clients become excited to meet their attorney instead of worried about whether they're making the right choice.

This isn't just about making clients feel better—though that's certainly important. This is about preventing buyer's remorse, reducing cancellations, building the kind of confidence that generates referrals, and creating the foundation for a strong attorney-client relationship from the very first interaction.

THE PSYCHOLOGY OF ATTORNEY ASSIGNMENT ANXIETY

Understanding why clients become anxious about attorney assignments helps you address their concerns proactively. When someone hires a firm rather than a specific attorney, several psychological factors create uncertainty and doubt.

Loss of Control and Agency

Criminal clients are already dealing with a situation where they feel powerless and out of control. When you assign them to an attorney they haven't chosen, it can trigger additional feelings of helplessness. They worry that they're being shuffled around or treated like just another case number.

Fear of Getting the "B Team"

Many clients assume that the person who handled their intake call was either the attorney or the firm's best representative. When they're told they'll work with someone else, they often worry they're being passed off to a less qualified or less experienced attorney.

Uncertainty About Personal Compatibility

Criminal representation is intensely personal. Clients need to trust their attorney with embarrassing details, rely on them during one of the most stressful periods of their lives, and feel confident that their attorney will fight for them. Without meeting the attorney first, they can't assess whether they'll have good personal chemistry.

Doubt About Decision Quality

If they're not confident about their assigned attorney, they start second-guessing their decision to hire your firm. This doubt can grow during the time between hiring and meeting the attorney, potentially leading to cancellations or requests for different representation.

THE "EXACTLY" LANGUAGE PATTERN

The foundation of effective preselling is a simple but powerful language pattern that eliminates doubt about case fit. Always use the word "exactly" when describing how well-suited your attorney is for their specific situation.

Wrong: "We handle DUI cases like yours."
Right: "This is exactly the type of case we handle every day."

Wrong: "Attorney Johnson has experience with these cases."
Right: "Attorney Johnson handles cases exactly like yours— this is right in his wheelhouse."

Wrong: "We've dealt with similar situations."
Right: "We've handled situations exactly like this hundreds of times."

The word "exactly" eliminates doubt and suggests perfect fit rather than general capability. When someone is scared and uncertain, "exactly" gives them confidence that they've found the right place and the right attorney for their specific situation.

This isn't about exaggeration or overselling. It's about using precise language that accurately conveys your firm's capability while building client confidence.

THE ATTORNEY PRESELLING FORMULA

When assigning an attorney, use this three-part formula consistently. The order matters because it mirrors how clients actually evaluate attorneys during crisis situations.

Part 1: Personal Qualities First

Start with who they are as a person, not what they've accomplished professionally. Criminal clients need to trust their attorney personally before they can appreciate their professional qualifications.

Effective personal quality statements:
- "Attorney Smith is incredibly patient and understanding."
- "She really takes time to explain everything clearly and never makes you feel rushed."
- "He's genuinely caring and will answer all your questions, no matter how many times you need to ask."
- "She makes sure you feel comfortable and never judges you for what happened."

These statements address the client's emotional needs first: the need to feel understood, respected, and supported during a difficult time.

Part 2: Professional Expertise Second

Once you've established personal compatibility, build their confidence in the attorney's professional capabilities.

Effective expertise statements:
- "He's been handling these specific types of cases for over 10 years."
- "She knows all the prosecutors and judges in this jurisdiction."
- "He has excellent relationships throughout the courthouse."
- "She's handled hundreds of cases exactly like yours with great results."

Notice that these statements are specific rather than general. "These specific types of cases" is more compelling than "criminal cases." "This jurisdiction" is more reassuring than "the local courts."

Part 3: Specific Local Knowledge Third

Finally, emphasize their courthouse advantages and local expertise.

Effective local knowledge statements:
- "He's in this courthouse every week and knows exactly how things work there."
- "She knows exactly how Judge Williams runs her courtroom and what approaches work best."
- "He understands what strategies are most effective with your specific prosecutor."
- "She has excellent working relationships with the court staff, which often helps with scheduling and logistics."

This sequence—personal qualities, professional expertise, then local knowledge—builds trust first, confidence second, and competitive advantage third.

COMPLETE PRESELLING SCRIPT EXAMPLE

Here's how the three-part formula sounds in practice:

"Based on what you've told me about your situation, I'm going to connect you with Attorney Johnson. He's perfect for your case because this is exactly the type of situation he handles.

You're going to really like working with him because he's one of our most patient and understanding attorneys. He really takes time to explain your options clearly and answer all your questions. You'll feel comfortable with him right away because he genuinely cares about his clients and makes sure you understand everything that's happening with your case.

He's also incredibly knowledgeable and experienced with these specific charges. He's been practicing criminal defense for 12 years and handles dozens of cases like yours every year. He knows all the ins and outs of these types of charges and exactly what defenses work best.

What's really valuable for your situation is that he's in your courthouse twice a week, so he knows all the prosecutors and judges personally. He has excellent working relationships there, which often helps in negotiations. Judge Martinez really respects his preparation and professionalism, and that benefits all his clients.

I'm going to have him call you within the next hour to walk you through your specific options. You're going to feel much better after talking with him."

Notice how this builds systematically: personal connection first, then expertise, then competitive advantage. By the end, they're looking forward to meeting their attorney rather than worried about the assignment.

THE APPOINTMENT BOOKING SYSTEM

How you handle the logistics of connecting clients with their assigned attorney either builds confidence or creates additional anxiety. Never leave clients wondering when, how, or if they'll hear from their attorney.

What Not to Say

"Our attorneys aren't available right now, but someone will call you back."

This creates multiple sources of anxiety:
- When will they call?
- Who specifically will call?
- Will they actually call?
- Should I wait by the phone?
- What if I miss the call?

The Systematic Booking Approach

Instead, use a systematic approach that eliminates uncertainty:

Immediate Team Communication
Message your team immediately to check attorney availability. Don't make clients wait while you figure out scheduling.

Specific Timing with Names
Give specific timing with the attorney's name:

- "I can have Daniel call you in 15 minutes."
- "Attorney Johnson can speak with you at 2 PM today."
- "Sarah will call you at 4:30 this afternoon."

Time Requirement Assessment
Ask about their availability: "How much time do you need to be free for Daniel to call? He'll want to go through your situation thoroughly, so plan on about 30 minutes."

Complete Booking Script

"Let me connect you with Daniel right now. I'm going to check his availability... [Check with team] Perfect! Daniel can call you in about 15 minutes. He'll have time to really go through your situation thoroughly and answer all your questions.

In the meantime, I'm sending you our courthouse guide for your specific court—it has everything you need to know about parking, where to meet your attorney, and what to expect. I'm also sending our first-offender guide that explains the process step by step.

So expect Daniel's call in 15 minutes, and you'll have those guides in your email within the next few minutes. Does that work for your schedule?"

Why This System Works

Eliminates Uncertainty: They know exactly when and who will call.

Creates Accountability: Specific person, specific time creates mutual commitment.

Provides Immediate Value: Courthouse guides and resources demonstrate organization and thoughtfulness.

Builds Confidence: The organized, professional process reinforces their decision to hire your firm.

Reduces Anxiety: Clear expectations and timeline prevent them from worrying about next steps.

SUPPORTING MATERIALS STRATEGY

Effective preselling goes beyond verbal descriptions. Supporting materials help clients feel informed and confident about their assigned attorney and upcoming representation.

Attorney Biography Videos

Each attorney should create a brief, personal video (maximum 10 minutes) covering:

Personal Background and Motivation
Why they chose criminal defense, what drives their passion for helping clients, personal connection to justice issues.

Professional Experience and Specialization
Years of experience, specific types of cases handled, areas of particular expertise or interest.

Local Knowledge and Relationships
Courthouse experience, relationships with prosecutors and judges, understanding of local procedures and preferences.

Client Service Philosophy
How they communicate with clients, their approach to explanation and education, availability and responsiveness standards.

Recent Successes (Without Violating Confidentiality)

General types of positive outcomes achieved, approach to difficult cases, problem-solving methodology.

These videos should feel conversational and personal rather than corporate or promotional. Clients should feel like they're meeting a real person who cares about their situation, not watching a marketing video.

Courthouse-Specific Guides

Create detailed, practical guides for each courthouse your firm serves:

Logistics Information:
- Parking options (free vs. paid, time limits, walking distances)
- Building entrance procedures and security requirements
- Restroom and water fountain locations
- Cell phone and electronic device policies

Meeting Information:
- Where to meet your attorney
- How early to arrive
- What to bring and what to leave at home
- Courtroom locations and procedures

Expectation Management:
- Typical timeline for different types of hearings
- What happens during various court proceedings
- How to dress and conduct yourself
- What family members need to know

Immediate Send Protocol

After assigning an attorney and booking the call, immediately send:

Attorney Bio Video Link: "Here's a brief video from Attorney Johnson so you can get to know him before your call."

Courthouse Guide PDF: "This guide has everything you need to know about your courthouse and what to expect."

Brief Email Message: "Here's some information about Attorney Johnson and what to expect. He'll be calling you at [specific time] to discuss your case in detail and answer all your questions."

This keeps clients engaged and builds anticipation for the attorney call instead of leaving them to worry about their decision during the waiting period.

ADVANCED PRESELLING TECHNIQUES

Addressing Specific Client Concerns

Tailor your preselling approach to address the specific concerns each client has expressed:

For clients worried about cost: Emphasize the attorney's efficiency and strategic approach that maximizes value.

For clients worried about outcome: Focus on the attorney's experience with similar cases and knowledge of what works in their jurisdiction.

For clients worried about communication: Highlight the attorney's responsiveness and commitment to keeping clients informed.

For clients worried about judgment: Emphasize the attorney's understanding, empathy, and non-judgmental approach.

Building Excitement Rather Than Just Reducing Anxiety

Instead of just addressing concerns, create positive anticipation:

"You're going to really enjoy working with Attorney Smith. Our clients consistently tell us how much they appreciate her thorough explanations and strategic thinking."

"Attorney Johnson has a great approach to cases like yours—he's going to help you understand options you probably haven't even considered yet."

Creating Connection Before Contact

Help clients feel like they already have a relationship with their attorney before they speak:

"Attorney Davis actually handled a very similar case just last month. She'll be able to share some insights about what worked well and what you can expect."

"You and Attorney Wilson are going to work well together. He has a very calm, methodical approach that really helps clients feel confident about their representation."

MEASURING PRESELLING EFFECTIVENESS

Track these metrics to ensure your preselling efforts are working:

Client Satisfaction Scores: Clients who are properly presold typically rate their satisfaction higher from the first attorney interaction.

Attorney-Client Relationship Quality: Attorneys report better initial meetings and stronger ongoing relationships when clients have been properly presold.

Cancellation Rates: Effective preselling should reduce cancellations between hiring and first attorney meeting.

Referral Generation: Clients who feel confident about their attorney assignment from the beginning are more likely to refer others.

Attorney Efficiency: When clients have realistic expectations and confidence in their attorney, initial meetings are more productive and focused.

CHAPTER SUMMARY

Preselling your attorneys and firm is crucial for eliminating client anxiety about attorney assignments and building confidence in their hiring decision. The process requires systematic language patterns, strategic information sharing, and careful attention to timing and logistics.

The "exactly" language pattern eliminates doubt about case fit by emphasizing perfect alignment between the client's needs and the attorney's capabilities.

The three-part preselling formula—personal qualities first, professional expertise second, local knowledge third—mirrors how clients actually evaluate attorneys during crisis situations.

Systematic appointment booking with specific timing and names eliminates uncertainty and builds confidence in your firm's organization and professionalism.

Supporting materials like attorney videos and courthouse guides provide immediate value while building anticipation for the attorney relationship.

When executed properly, preselling transforms attorney assignment from a source of anxiety into a source of confidence and excitement. Clients feel informed, prepared, and confident about their choice rather than uncertain about their decision.

In the next chapter, we'll address the three most common objections that can derail even the best preselling efforts: price concerns, timing issues, and the dreaded "I need to think about it." You'll learn specific techniques for addressing each objection while maintaining the trust and confidence you've built through effective rapport building and preselling.

CHAPTER 5:

OVERCOMING THE BIG THREE OBJECTIONS

Here's something that might surprise you: the three objections that kill 80% of potential retainers are completely predictable. I can tell you right now exactly what your next ten potential clients are going to say when you get to the hiring discussion.

"I need to talk to my spouse."
"All lawyers are the same."
"That's a lot of money."

Most attorneys hear these objections and think the conversation is over. They either get defensive, start justifying their fees, or worse—they give up and hope the client calls back. Some attorneys actually end the call when they hear certain objections, assuming the prospect isn't serious about hiring them.

This is a fundamental misunderstanding of what objections actually represent. When someone gives you an objection, they're not saying "no." They're saying "I'm interested, but I need you to help me get comfortable with this decision."

Objections are actually buying signals and engagement opportunities. They indicate that the prospect is seriously considering hiring you but needs additional information, reassurance, or support to move forward. When you handle objections correctly, they actually move you closer to the retainer, not further away.

The key insight that transforms how you handle objections is this: address the psychology behind the objection, not just the surface-level concern. Each objection represents deeper emotional and psychological needs that must be understood and addressed systematically.

OBJECTION #1: "I NEED TO TALK TO MY SPOUSE/PARTNER"

This is the objection that kills more deals than any other, and it's the one that most attorneys handle most poorly. Here's what most attorneys don't realize: this objection is rarely about getting permission from a spouse. It's about complex psychological needs that go far beyond decision-making authority.

Understanding the Real Psychology

Post-Arrest Emotional Overwhelm Creates Decision Paralysis

They just experienced one of the most traumatic events of their life. Making a major financial decision while in emotional crisis feels overwhelming and potentially dangerous. They need time to process their situation and regain some sense of control over their life.

Fear of Disappointing Loved Ones and Family Shame

They're already embarrassed about getting arrested. Now they have to tell their spouse that they need to spend thousands of dollars to fix their mistake. They're dreading that conversation and hoping their spouse will somehow make the decision easier or less painful.

Need for Emotional Support in Major Decision-Making

This isn't just about getting advice—it's about needing emotional support from someone who loves them unconditionally. They want reassurance that they're making the right choice and that their family will support them through this difficult period.

Legitimate Financial Decision Authority and Consultation

Sometimes this genuinely is about shared financial decision-making in relationships where major expenses require mutual agreement. This is the least common reason, but it does occur.

Wrong Response Approaches

Never Ask "How Long Will That Conversation Take?"

This sounds pushy and dismissive of their relationship dynamics. It suggests that you're more concerned about closing the deal than respecting their decision-making process.

Never Say "We Really Need to Move Quickly on This"

You're adding pressure to someone who's already overwhelmed. Even when there are legitimate timing concerns, this approach typically backfires by triggering their fight-or-flight response.

Never Say "They Don't Understand Legal Matters Like You Do"

This insults their spouse and creates conflict in their relationship. You're essentially asking them to choose between your advice and their partner's input, which is a losing proposition.

Any form of pressure or minimization will backfire completely because it invalidates their emotional needs and relationship priorities.

The Right Response Framework

Use this four-step framework to address the psychology behind this objection:

Validate: "Of course you want to discuss this important decision with them. That makes perfect sense, and I'd be concerned if you didn't want to talk it over."

Normalize: "Most people want their family's input on major decisions like this. It shows you value their perspective and want them to feel comfortable with this choice."

Facilitate: "What specific information would help you have that conversation effectively? I want to make sure you have everything you need to discuss this thoroughly."

Bridge: "I'd be happy to speak with both of you together if that would be helpful. Sometimes spouses have different questions or concerns than the person who was arrested."

Advanced Techniques for This Objection

Offer Direct Spouse Communication

"Would it be helpful if I explained our approach directly to your wife so she can ask any questions she might have? Sometimes spouses are more comfortable when they can speak with the attorney themselves."

This removes you as the middleman and allows the spouse to get direct answers to their concerns. It also demonstrates confidence in your ability to address any objections they might raise.

Provide Written Summary Documentation

"Let me email you a detailed summary of what we discussed today, including our approach, what's included in our representation, and the timeline we're looking at. That way you can share specific information rather than trying to remember everything from our conversation."

This gives them concrete information to share and prevents miscommunication or forgotten details that could derail the spousal conversation.

Set Specific Follow-Up Timeline

"Why don't we plan to talk tomorrow evening after you've had a chance to discuss this thoroughly? That gives you time for a proper conversation without feeling rushed."

This respects their process while maintaining momentum and accountability.

Proactively Address Spouse's Likely Concerns

"She's probably going to wonder about the cost and whether this is really necessary. Let me give you some specific points to help address those concerns..."

Then provide them with clear, logical arguments that address common spousal objections about legal expenses and necessity of private representation.

OBJECTION #2: "ALL LAWYERS ARE THE SAME"

This objection makes most attorneys immediately defensive, but it's crucial not to take it personally. This is about their perception of the legal industry based on advertising, media portrayals, and possibly previous experiences with attorneys in other practice areas.

Understanding the Real Issues

Commoditization of Legal Services in Public Perception

Legal advertising often makes attorneys sound identical—everyone claims to be experienced, aggressive, and client-focused. From the outside, it can seem like every lawyer says exactly the same things about their services.

Previous Negative Experiences with Attorneys

They may have hired a lawyer for a divorce, real estate transaction, or personal injury case who disappointed them. They're projecting that experience onto all attorneys, including criminal defense specialists.

Lack of Understanding About Criminal Defense Specialization

They don't realize that criminal law is completely different from other practice areas, requiring different skills, relationships, and approaches. They think legal work is legal work.

Price Shopping Mentality Without Value Comprehension

They're comparing lawyers like they'd compare plumbers or mechanics—assuming the service is identical and price should be the only differentiator.

Wrong Response Approaches

Don't Immediately List Credentials and Awards

This actually proves their point that all lawyers say the same things. Every attorney they call will mention their experience, education, and accolades.

Don't Criticize Other Attorneys

This makes you look unprofessional and petty. It also suggests that you can't compete on your own merits.

Don't Give Generic "We're Different" Statements

Everyone says they're different. Without specific proof points, this statement is meaningless.

Don't Get Defensive

Defensiveness kills rapport and makes you sound insecure about your value proposition.

The Right Response Framework

Acknowledge: "I understand why it might seem that way from the outside. There's a lot of confusing legal advertising out there, and much of it does sound very similar."

Educate: "Here's what you should actually look for when choosing criminal defense counsel..." Then provide specific criteria they can use to evaluate attorneys.

Differentiate: "Let me explain our specific approach to cases like yours and how it differs from what you might find elsewhere."

Demonstrate: "Here's exactly what you can expect from our process, and here's how you can verify that we deliver on these promises."

Specific Differentiation Points

Geographic Coverage vs. Limited Practice

"We handle cases in all Connecticut courts, not just local municipalities. This means we understand how different judges and prosecutors approach cases throughout the state."

Criminal Defense Specialization vs. General Practice

"We only do criminal defense. We don't handle divorces, real estate, or personal injury cases. This focused specialization means we stay current on criminal law changes and maintain relationships with the people who matter for your case."

Dedicated Support Team vs. Attorney-Only Handling

"You'll have a whole team working on your case—paralegals, investigators, and support staff—not just one overworked attorney trying to handle everything alone."

Advanced Technology and Communication Systems

"You'll never wonder what's happening with your case. Our case management system keeps you informed every step of the way."

Transparent Flat Fee Structure vs. Hourly Billing Uncertainty

"You know exactly what this will cost upfront. No surprise bills, no hourly charges that spiral out of control."

OBJECTION #3: COST SHOCK AND STICKER SHOCK

This is where most attorneys completely sabotage their positioning. They either get defensive about their fees or immediately start offering payment plans before building value. Both approaches destroy your credibility and positioning.

Understanding the Real Psychology

Complete Lack of Frame of Reference

Most people have no idea what legal services actually cost. They think hiring a lawyer should be like hiring someone to fix a speeding ticket—a few hundred dollars at most.

Financial Stress Compounded by Arrest Consequences

They're worried about losing income, losing their job, dealing with insurance issues, and now they're facing a major unexpected expense.

Inappropriate Comparison Points

They're comparing criminal defense representation to traffic ticket attorneys, divorce lawyers who advertise low flat fees, or other legal services that aren't comparable to criminal defense.

Fear of Ongoing Costs and Hidden Fees

They're afraid the initial fee is just the beginning—that the $5,000 will become $15,000 through additional costs and unexpected charges.

Wrong Response Approaches

Don't Immediately Justify Your Price Without Building Value

This sounds defensive and suggests that you're not confident about your value proposition.

Don't Offer Payment Plans Before Explaining Value

This cheapens your positioning and suggests that you expect people to have trouble affording your services.

Don't Compare Your Prices to Other Attorneys

You're not competing on price. You're competing on value and outcomes.

Don't Use an Apologetic or Defensive Tone

Your fees are what they are for legitimate business reasons. Apologizing for them undermines your credibility.

The Right Response Framework

Acknowledge: "I know this represents a significant investment, and I want to make sure you understand exactly what's at stake and what this covers."

Reframe: "Let's talk about what we're actually solving for you and what the alternatives might cost you long-term."

Value Build: "Here's everything that's included in our comprehensive representation..." Then detail every aspect of your service.

Consequences: "Here's what could potentially happen without proper representation..." Discuss both legal and collateral consequences.

Cost Justification Techniques

Break Down Total Value Delivered

"This covers everything from the initial investigation through final resolution—all court appearances, all negotiations with prosecutors, all communication with you throughout the process, and any appeals if necessary."

Compare Investment to Long-Term Consequences

"A conviction could cost you your job, your professional license, your ability to get certain loans or housing. We're not just defending against these charges—we're protecting your future earning capacity."

Explain Flat Fee Benefits

"You never have to worry about getting an unexpected bill. Whether your case resolves in three months or takes a year, your cost remains the same."

Present Flexible Payment Options Without Compromising Positioning

"We have several options to make this work within your budget. The important thing is getting you proper representation."

ADVANCED OBJECTION HANDLING TECHNIQUES

The Feel, Felt, Found Method

This classic technique works because it creates emotional connection while providing logical resolution:

"I understand how you feel about this—it's a significant decision and a major investment. Other clients have felt the same way when they first called us, uncertain about whether they really needed private representation. Here's what they found after working with our team..."

Then share specific examples (maintaining confidentiality) of how your representation made a difference in outcomes and client satisfaction.

Preemptive Objection Handling

The best way to handle objections is to address them before they're raised:

Build Value Proactively

Explain your process and what's included before discussing fees. When people understand the scope of representation, the investment makes more sense.

Set Proper Expectations Early

"Most people are surprised by legal costs because they don't realize everything that goes into proper criminal defense representation. Let me walk you through what's involved..."

Address Common Concerns Upfront

"You're probably wondering whether all lawyers handle these cases the same way. Let me explain what makes criminal defense representation effective..."

When to Stop Responding to Objections

Sometimes people aren't objecting because they're genuinely concerned—they're objecting because they're not ready to make any decision. Learning to recognize this difference is crucial for time management and conversion optimization.

Recognize Genuine Interest vs. Endless Objection Cycling

If they keep coming up with new objections after you've thoroughly addressed the original ones, they're probably not ready to hire anyone. They may need more time to process their situation.

Move Forward When Objections Become Delay Tactics

"It sounds like you might need some time to think about this overall situation. What would be most helpful for you right now—taking some time to process everything, or would you prefer to schedule a time to continue this conversation when you're ready?"

This gracefully exits the conversation while keeping the door open for future contact.

PRACTICE SCENARIOS

Combination Objections

Prospect: "I need to talk to my wife, and honestly, this seems like a lot of money for something that might not even help."

Response: "Absolutely, you should discuss this with your wife—this affects your whole family, not just you. And I want her to feel confident about this investment too. Let me give you some specific information to share with her about what's included in our representation and what the alternatives might cost you long-term. I think once she understands what's at stake and how we protect families in situations like this, she'll feel much better about moving forward."

Hostile Objection Delivery

Prospect: "Are you kidding me? Five thousand dollars? All lawyers are just trying to rip people off!"

Response: "I can hear how frustrated and overwhelmed you are, and I completely understand why this feels like a lot right now. You're dealing with something you never expected to face, and now there are all these costs and decisions to make. Let me help you understand what goes into handling a case like this properly, and then you can decide if it makes sense for your situation. Fair enough?"

Multiple Decision Makers

Prospect: "My parents are paying for this, so they need to approve anything we do."

Response: "That makes perfect sense, and it's great that your parents are supporting you through this. Would it be helpful if I spoke with all three of you together so everyone can ask questions and feel comfortable with the decision? I want your parents to feel confident that their investment is protecting your future properly."

MEASURING OBJECTION HANDLING EFFECTIVENESS

Track these metrics to improve your objection handling skills:

Objection-to-Conversion Ratios: How often do prospects who raise objections eventually hire you?

Objection Type Patterns: Which objections appear most frequently, and how has your handling improved over time?

Follow-Up Success Rates: When prospects need time to think or consult others, how often do they return to hire you?

Call Duration After Objections: Effective objection handling should extend conversations and deepen engagement rather than ending them.

CHAPTER SUMMARY

The three most common objections in criminal defense intake are predictable and addressable when you understand the psychology behind them. Each objection represents genuine concerns that must be validated and systematically addressed rather than overcome through pressure or defensiveness.

"I need to talk to my spouse" is rarely about permission—it's about emotional overwhelm, family shame, and need for support. Address this through validation, facilitation, and offering direct spouse communication.

"All lawyers are the same" reflects industry commoditization and lack of understanding about criminal defense specialization. Address this through education about what differentiates effective criminal representation and specific proof points about your approach.

"That's a lot of money" stems from lack of reference points and fear of ongoing costs. Address this by building value first, reframing the investment in terms of consequences avoided, and providing transparent cost structures.

Advanced techniques include preemptive objection handling, the feel-felt-found method, and recognizing when objections become delay tactics rather than genuine concerns.

When handled properly, objections become opportunities to deepen trust, provide education, and move closer to retainer agreements. The key is addressing the underlying psychology rather than just the surface-level concerns.

In the next chapter, we'll explore the art of closing without being pushy—how to guide prospects to hiring decisions while respecting their autonomy and maintaining the trust you've built throughout the intake process.

CHAPTER 6:

THE VALUE PROPOSITION THAT CONVERTS

Here's a hard truth that most attorneys refuse to accept: expertise and credentials alone don't sell legal services. I've watched brilliant lawyers with impressive credentials consistently lose clients to attorneys with half their experience and twice their fees.

Why does this happen? Because they made a fundamental mistake—they confused being qualified with being valuable.

Your potential clients don't care that you graduated summa cum laude from law school. They don't care that you've been practicing for twenty years. They don't even care that you've won 500 cases. What they care about is one simple question: Will you solve their problem and protect what matters most to them?

This distinction is crucial for understanding why so many technically excellent attorneys struggle with intake conversion. They spend their conversations listing accomplishments, reciting credentials, and explaining their experience. Meanwhile, prospects are thinking about losing their jobs, disappointing their families, and navigating an unfamiliar legal system that feels designed to overwhelm them.

There's a critical difference between features, benefits, and true value that most attorneys never learn:

Features are what you do: "I handle criminal defense cases."
Benefits are what clients get: "You get experienced representation."
Value is how their life is better: "You protect your career and keep your family secure."

When you understand this progression and learn to communicate value rather than features, price becomes secondary to the protection you provide. Clients stop shopping around and start focusing on getting the best possible outcome for their situation.

THE EXPERTISE TRAP THAT KILLS CONVERSIONS

Most attorneys fall into what I call the "expertise trap"—the belief that demonstrating qualifications automatically creates confidence and trust. In reality, leading with credentials often creates distance and intimidation rather than connection and comfort.

Why Listing Credentials Creates Distance

When you open a conversation by listing your law school, your awards, and your bar admissions, you're essentially saying "I'm impressive and you should be impressed." But clients in crisis don't need to be impressed—they need to feel safe and protected.

Consider the psychological state of someone who just got arrested. They feel small, powerless, and judged. When you immediately establish how accomplished and impressive you are, you're inadvertently emphasizing the power differential between you. Instead of feeling reassured, they often feel more intimidated and uncertain about whether they're important enough for your attention.

How Expertise Can Intimidate Rather Than Attract

If you sound too polished, too accomplished, or too important, prospects start wondering whether you'll really care about their "small" DUI case when you've handled major felonies. They worry that they're wasting your time or that their case isn't significant enough to warrant your full attention.

This is particularly problematic with first-time offenders who are already embarrassed about their situation. They don't want to feel like they're bothering a "big shot" attorney with their relatively minor case.

Making Expertise Accessible and Relevant

Instead of listing general credentials, make your experience directly relevant to their specific situation:

Instead of: "I've been practicing criminal law for 15 years."
Say: "I've helped hundreds of people in situations exactly like yours."

Instead of: "I graduated from Yale Law School."
Say: "I understand exactly what you're going through and how to protect your future."

The difference is that the first approach is about you and your accomplishments. The second approach is about them and their needs.

VALUE-BASED POSITIONING FRAMEWORK

Effective value positioning requires a fundamental shift from describing what you do to articulating what clients achieve by working with you. This framework helps you consistently communicate value rather than features.

Outcome Focus: What Client Achieves vs. What Attorney Does

Traditional Approach: "I file motions and negotiate with prosecutors."
Value-Based Approach: "You get your life back on track and move forward with confidence."

Traditional Approach: "I provide comprehensive legal representation."
Value-Based Approach: "You get peace of mind knowing every aspect of your case is handled by experts."

The outcome focus puts the client at the center of the conversation and helps them visualize the positive results of hiring you.

Risk Mitigation: What Client Avoids vs. What Attorney Prevents

Traditional Approach: "I handle professional licensing issues."
Value-Based Approach: "You avoid losing your professional license and protect your career."

Traditional Approach: "I work to minimize charges."
Value-Based Approach: "You avoid the conviction that could follow you for decades."

Risk mitigation speaks to their deepest fears and positions you as protection against their worst-case scenarios.

Peace of Mind: How Client Feels vs. What Attorney Provides

Traditional Approach: "I provide regular case updates."
Value-Based Approach: "You sleep at night knowing an expert is handling every detail."

Traditional Approach: "I have extensive trial experience."
Value-Based Approach: "You feel confident that if your case goes to trial, you have the best possible advocate."

Peace of mind addresses the emotional benefits of your representation, which often matter more to clients than technical legal benefits.

Future Protection: Long-Term Benefits vs. Immediate Services

Traditional Approach: "I represent you in court."
Value-Based Approach: "This protects your career and reputation for decades to come."

Traditional Approach: "I negotiate with prosecutors."
Value-Based Approach: "You preserve opportunities for your family's future."

Future protection helps clients understand that they're not just buying representation for their current case—they're investing in their long-term wellbeing.

PRICE VS. VALUE POSITIONING

One of the biggest mistakes attorneys make is competing on price rather than positioning based on value. When you compete on price, you commoditize your services and attract clients who will leave you for anyone cheaper.

Investment vs. Cost Language Patterns

Instead of: "Our fee is $5,000."
Say: "This is an investment in protecting everything you've worked to build."

Instead of: "Legal representation costs money."
Say: "You're investing in your future and your family's security."

The word "investment" implies return and value, while "cost" implies expense and burden.

Total Cost of Inadequate Representation

Help clients understand that the cheapest option often becomes the most expensive:

"The real cost isn't just the attorney's fee—it's the conviction that follows you for the rest of your life. It's the job opportunities you lose, the professional licenses that get revoked, the background checks that come back with criminal records."

"When you hire inadequate representation, you might save money upfront, but you pay for it for years through consequences that proper representation could have prevented."

Reframing Expense as Protection and Insurance

"Think of this as insurance for your future. You pay a premium now to protect against catastrophic loss later. Just like you wouldn't buy the cheapest car insurance when you have a valuable car, you shouldn't buy the cheapest legal representation when your future is at stake."

Positioning Statement for Price Concerns

"We're not the cheapest option, and here's why that's actually good for you. When your future is on the line, you want the attorney who's going to fight hardest for the best outcome, not the one with the lowest fee. Cheap legal representation is expensive when it doesn't work."

THE "YOU DON'T GO TO COURT ALONE" CORE MESSAGING

This positioning statement works because it addresses the fundamental fear every criminal defendant has—facing the system alone. It's emotional, memorable, and differentiating.

Message Development Strategy

Balance Emotional Appeals with Logical Support

Lead with emotional connection, then support with logical arguments:

"You're scared and confused right now, and that's completely normal. Here's exactly how we're going to help you navigate this process and protect your future."

Address Fear and Provide Hope

Acknowledge what they're afraid of losing, then show them the path to protecting it:

"I know you're worried about losing your job. Here's how we protect your employment while we handle your case."

Focus on Support Rather Than Just Services

You're not just providing legal services—you're providing human support during the worst time of their life:

"You're not just getting an attorney. You're getting a whole team of people who understand what you're going through and know how to help."

The Three Core Message Pillars

Pillar 1: Expertise in Your Corner

"You get trained advocates who understand the system and all the players involved. We have years of experience handling cases exactly like yours—we know what works and what doesn't. We have established relationships with prosecutors and judges that can benefit your case, and we understand the specific procedures and personalities in your courthouse."

Pillar 2: Comprehensive Support Throughout the Process

"We handle every detail so you can focus on your life and your family. No surprises—we explain everything as we move forward so you always know what's happening. We're available when questions or concerns arise—you're never left wondering what's going on. Complete guidance from start to finish—you never have to figure out what to do next."

Pillar 3: Proven Process and Track Record

"We have a systematic approach that's worked for hundreds of clients in similar situations. Clear next steps and realistic timeline expectations—no false promises or unrealistic hopes. Track record of favorable outcomes because we know how to position your case effectively. Transparency in our process and communication throughout—you always know where you stand."

Language That Creates Emotional Connection

"Having someone experienced in your corner when everything feels uncertain."

"You're not facing this challenging situation alone anymore."

"We'll fight for your future and what matters most to you and your family."

"Protecting not just your case, but your life, your career, and your reputation."

DIFFERENTIATING FROM PUBLIC DEFENDERS AND CIVIL ATTORNEYS

Many attorneys make the mistake of criticizing public defenders or civil attorneys to differentiate themselves. This approach is unprofessional and unnecessary. You can differentiate respectfully while highlighting your advantages.

Public Defender Differentiation (Without Criticism)

Time and Personal Attention Difference:

"Individual focus versus overwhelming caseload demands—we have time to really dive deep into your case and explore every possible defense."

"Available when you need guidance and have questions—you're not competing for attention with 100 other cases."

"Personalized strategy for your specific situation—not a one-size-fits-all approach."

Choice and Control in Your Representation:

"You choose your advocate instead of being assigned someone you've never met."

"Direct communication with your attorney—not filtered through overloaded court staff."

"Flexibility in approach and strategy development—we adapt our approach to what works best for your situation."

Civil Attorney Differentiation

Criminal Law Specialization Advantages:

"This is all we do, every single day—criminal defense is our complete focus."

"Deep expertise in criminal procedure and strategy—we know the nuances that make the difference between conviction and dismissal."

"Established relationships with criminal court personnel—prosecutors, judges, court staff who handle cases like yours."

"Experience with hundreds of cases like yours—we've seen every variation of your situation and know what works."

Respectful Positioning Statements

"While public defenders do important and necessary work, we can provide individual attention and personalized strategy that's difficult with their caseloads."

"Civil attorneys are excellent in their areas, but criminal defense requires specialized knowledge and relationships that come from exclusive focus on criminal law."

"You deserve representation from someone whose complete focus is criminal defense and protecting people in situations exactly like yours."

VALUE COMMUNICATION TECHNIQUES

Story-Based Value Demonstration

Use client success stories to illustrate outcomes while maintaining confidentiality:

"I had another client last month with very similar charges and a similar situation. Here's what we were able to accomplish for him..."

Create before-and-after scenarios that show transformation:

"When he first called us, he was convinced his career was over and his family would never forgive him. Six months later, the charges were dismissed, he got promoted at work, and his family was stronger than ever."

Share process stories that demonstrate thoroughness and care:

"Let me walk you through exactly what happened with another client's case so you can see how we approach these situations systematically."

Consequence-Focused Messaging

Help clients understand what's truly at stake beyond just potential jail time:

"This isn't just about avoiding jail—it's about protecting everything you've worked to build. A conviction follows you on background checks, affects professional licensing, impacts housing applications, and can even affect your children's opportunities."

Emphasize long-term impact beyond the immediate case:

"We're not just defending against these charges—we're protecting your future earning capacity, your professional reputation, and your family's financial security."

Focus on family and career protection:

"This isn't just about you—it's about protecting your family's financial security and your children's future opportunities. When we take your case, we're fighting for everyone who depends on you."

PRACTICAL VALUE PROPOSITION EXAMPLES

Traditional Approach vs. Value-Based Approach

Instead of:
"I'm an experienced criminal defense attorney with 15 years of experience and a track record of success in criminal defense cases."

Say this:
"You get an advocate who's handled hundreds of cases like yours and knows exactly how to protect your job, your reputation, and your future. You're not going to court alone— you're going with someone who fights for your best interests every step of the way."

Instead of:
"Our firm handles all types of criminal cases and has extensive experience in criminal defense."

Say this:
"This is all we do—protect people who find themselves facing criminal charges. We know the prosecutors, we understand the judges, and we have a proven process for getting the best possible outcome in your specific situation."

Instead of:
"We provide comprehensive legal representation and client service."

Say this:
"You get peace of mind knowing that every detail is handled by experts who care about your outcome. You'll never wonder what's happening with your case or what you should do next— we guide you through everything."

The difference is transformational. The first approach focuses on you and your qualifications. The second approach focuses on them and what they achieve by working with you.

MEASURING VALUE PROPOSITION EFFECTIVENESS

Track these metrics to ensure your value positioning is working:

Reduced Price Shopping: Clients who understand your value are less likely to call multiple attorneys comparing prices.

Shorter Sales Cycles: When prospects understand value clearly, they make decisions faster.

Higher Conversion Rates: Value-focused conversations convert at higher rates than credential-focused conversations.

Client Satisfaction Scores: Clients who hired you based on value rather than price are typically more satisfied with representation.

Referral Generation: Clients who understand your value are more likely to refer others facing similar situations.

CHAPTER SUMMARY

Effective value positioning transforms how prospects perceive your services and makes price secondary to protection. The key insights for creating compelling value propositions are:

Expertise alone doesn't sell—transformation and protection sell. Clients hire attorneys who can solve their problems and protect what matters most to them.

Lead with what they get, not what you do. Focus on outcomes, risk mitigation, peace of mind, and future protection rather than credentials and experience.

Make credentials relevant to their specific situation. Instead of listing general qualifications, connect your experience directly to their needs and fears.

Position yourself as advocate, not vendor. You're not selling legal services—you're providing protection, peace of mind, and a better future.

Differentiate respectfully without criticizing competitors. Highlight your advantages through positive positioning rather than negative comparisons.

Use story-based demonstration and consequence-focused messaging to help prospects understand what's truly at stake and visualize positive outcomes.

When you master value positioning, price objections disappear because clients understand they're not buying legal services— they're investing in protection and peace of mind. They stop comparing you to other attorneys because they recognize you're solving their problem in a way nobody else can.

In the next chapter, we'll explore the art of closing without being pushy—how to guide prospects to hiring decisions using consultative techniques that feel natural and respectful while maintaining the trust you've built throughout the intake process.

CHAPTER 7:

CLOSING WITHOUT BEING PUSHY

Most attorneys struggle with closing for a simple but critical reason: traditional sales closing techniques fail catastrophically in criminal defense. The high-pressure, "always be closing" approach that might work in other industries will destroy your credibility with criminal clients faster than any other mistake you can make.

Consider the psychological state of your potential client. They just went through one of the most stressful experiences of their life. They're already feeling pressured, overwhelmed, and vulnerable. The last thing they need is an attorney who sounds like an aggressive salesperson trying to force them into a decision they're not ready to make.

But here's the problem that many well-intentioned attorneys face: if you don't guide prospects to a decision, they'll often stay stuck in analysis paralysis, shop around endlessly, or worse— hire someone less qualified who pushes them harder toward a quick decision.

The solution lies in understanding that there's a profound difference between creating legitimate urgency and applying manipulative pressure. You need to shift from a salesperson mindset to a consultant approach that respects their psychology while still moving them toward the protection they desperately need.

The key insight that transforms closing effectiveness is this: when you've properly built rapport, demonstrated value, and addressed concerns throughout the intake process, closing becomes a natural conversation about next steps rather than a high-pressure sales pitch.

THE CONSULTATIVE CLOSE FOR CRIMINAL DEFENSE

The consultative closing approach works because it aligns with how people in crisis actually make important decisions. Instead of trying to overcome resistance, you're guiding them to reach the logical conclusion that hiring you serves their best interests.

Consultation vs. Sales Mindset Shift

Leading Client to Logical Conclusion Rather Than Forcing Decision

You're not convincing them to hire you—you're helping them understand why hiring you makes the most sense for their specific situation. This subtle but important distinction changes your entire approach and energy.

Collaborative Decision-Making That Builds Trust

"Let's figure out the best path forward together" versus "You need to make a decision right now." The first approach invites partnership; the second creates pressure and resistance.

Focusing on Client Needs vs. Attorney Business Needs

Every aspect of your closing should center on their timeline, their concerns, and their decision-making process—not your need to close deals or fill your calendar.

Creating Partnership Rather Than Vendor Relationship

By the time you reach the closing phase, they should feel like you're already on their team, advocating for their interests rather than trying to sell them something.

The Three-Question Close Framework

This framework respects client autonomy while systematically moving toward a hiring decision. Each question serves a specific psychological purpose in the decision-making process.

Question 1: "Based on everything we've discussed, what makes the most sense to you?"

This question puts decision ownership with the client where it belongs. It assumes they've been engaged and listening throughout the conversation. It opens dialogue rather than forcing a binary yes/no response, and it allows them to verbalize their own reasoning for hiring you.

When clients articulate their own reasons for moving forward, they become more committed to the decision than if you had simply convinced them through persuasion.

Question 2: "What additional information do you need to move forward confidently?"

This question identifies any remaining genuine objections or concerns while demonstrating your continued willingness to educate and inform. It positions you as a resource and advisor rather than a vendor pushing for a sale.

This question also shows patience and a client-focused approach, which builds additional trust even during the closing phase.

Question 3: "What would you like to see happen next?"

This final question allows the client to choose and control the next steps while creating a natural transition to the retainer process. It maintains the collaborative approach throughout and respects their decision-making timeline.

Advanced Consultative Closing Techniques

The Assumption Close

"When we get started, the first step will be to review all the discovery materials, and then we'll develop our defense strategy from there."

This technique assumes they've decided to hire you and focuses on what happens next. It works when you've built strong rapport and addressed their primary concerns.

The Summary Close

"Let me make sure I understand what's most important to you— protecting your job, keeping this off your record, and making sure your family doesn't have to worry about this anymore. Is that right?"

This technique confirms their priorities and demonstrates that you've been listening throughout the conversation. It also allows you to position your services as the solution to their specific concerns.

CREATING URGENCY WITHOUT PRESSURE

One of the biggest challenges in criminal defense closing is creating appropriate urgency without triggering the fight-or-flight response that pressure tactics cause. The solution is to focus on legitimate urgency factors that serve the client's interests.

Legitimate Urgency Factors in Criminal Defense

Court Deadlines and Statutory Timing Requirements

"Your arraignment is next Monday, so we need to get started this week to properly prepare and make sure you're not going in there without representation."

This creates real urgency based on actual deadlines that affect case outcomes.

Evidence Preservation and Witness Availability

"The longer we wait, the more likely it is that video evidence gets recorded over or witnesses become harder to locate. Early action often preserves important evidence."

This urgency factor focuses on protecting their interests rather than serving your business needs.

Prosecutor Caseload Realities and Plea Negotiation Windows

"Early intervention often gives us more leverage in negotiations because prosecutors haven't locked into a position yet. Once they've invested time building their case, they become less flexible."

This educates them about how the system works while creating legitimate reasons to act promptly.

Procedural Deadline Concerns

"There are specific deadlines for filing certain motions, and missing them can eliminate defense options that might be crucial for your case."

This urgency is based on legal realities that genuinely affect case outcomes.

Urgency Communication Techniques

Deadline-Based Urgency

"Your arraignment is Monday, so we need to get the retainer handled by Friday so I can review everything over the weekend and be fully prepared."

Consequence-Based Urgency

"The sooner we start working on this, the more options we typically have available for building your defense."

Resource-Based Urgency

"I have availability this week to focus on your case immediately, but my calendar fills up pretty quickly with court appearances."

Opportunity-Based Urgency

"Early intervention often leads to significantly better outcomes because we can shape the narrative before positions get entrenched."

Avoiding Pressure Tactics That Backfire

Never Create False Deadlines or Artificial Scarcity

Criminal clients are already skeptical of attorneys and the legal system. Any hint of manipulation will destroy the trust you've worked to build.

Don't Use Emotional Manipulation or Fear Tactics

They're already afraid. Adding additional fear through manipulation will trigger their defenses and make them want to escape the conversation.

Avoid Making Your Availability the Primary Urgency Factor

"You need to decide today because I'm really busy" sounds self-serving and suggests that your schedule is more important than their decision-making process.

Focus on Their Timeline and Needs

All urgency should center on what serves their interests, not your business requirements.

THE STRATEGIC PRICING PAUSE TECHNIQUE

One of the most powerful closing techniques involves how you handle price discussions. When someone asks about your fees, you must pause and allow them to mentally prepare for the investment level.

The Psychology Behind the Pause

Most prospects have zero price awareness for criminal defense services, but they already know lawyers are expensive. When you pause after they ask "How much does this cost?" their mind immediately starts guessing at possible amounts.

This psychological preparation is crucial because it prevents sticker shock and makes your actual fees seem more reasonable.

Why This Technique Works

If you quote $8,500 and they were mentally preparing for $10,000, the difference feels like a discount. But if you don't give them time to think and you go directly from zero to $8,500, that's a massive psychological jump that can trigger price shock.

The Implementation Process

Client: "So how much is this going to cost?"

You: "Well, I have to warn you, comprehensive criminal defense representation is a significant investment..." [PAUSE for 3-4 seconds to let them think]

You: "For a case like yours, our fee is typically $8,500."

What Happens During the Pause

Their brain starts working: "Lawyers are expensive... this is serious... probably several thousand... maybe $5,000? Could be $10,000 or more..."

When you finally state your fee, you're either a bargain compared to what they imagined, or you're close enough that the difference doesn't feel shocking.

WHEN TO STOP TALKING AND ASK FOR THE RETAINER

Recognizing buying signals and knowing when to transition from consultation to commitment is crucial for closing effectiveness. Many attorneys talk past the close and actually convince prospects out of hiring them.

Buying Signals to Watch and Listen For

Questions About Process and Next Steps

"What happens after I hire you?" or "How long does this usually take?" These questions indicate they're thinking beyond the hiring decision to the actual representation.

Concerns About Specific Outcomes

"Will this affect my security clearance?" They're thinking about long-term implications, which suggests serious consideration of hiring you.

Timeline and Scheduling Discussions

"I have a work trip next month, will that be a problem?" They're trying to coordinate their life around your representation.

Questions About What's Included

"Does that cover everything through trial if necessary?" They're evaluating the complete value proposition.

Spouse or Family Involvement

"Can you explain this to my wife so she understands what we're dealing with?" They're bringing decision-makers into the process.

The Strategic Power of Silence

After Asking for Commitment

"Are you ready to get started protecting your future?" [SILENCE—let them process and respond]

Don't fill the silence with additional selling. Give them space to make their decision.

After Stating Investment Amount

"The fee for comprehensive representation is $7,500." [SILENCE—allow absorption time]

Let them process the investment level before you say anything else.

After Presenting Payment Options

"The total investment is $8,500. Are you able to handle that today?" [SILENCE]

If they hesitate, then offer: "We do have payment plan options if that would be more manageable for your situation."

Retainer Request Language

Direct Approach

"We'd like to represent you in this matter. Are you ready to get started protecting your future?"

Assumption Approach

"Let's get your retainer handled so we can begin working on your defense immediately."

Collaborative Approach

"Based on everything we've discussed, it sounds like moving forward makes sense. What would you like to do next?"

HANDLING THE "LET ME THINK ABOUT IT" RESPONSE

This response is inevitable in criminal defense intake, and how you handle it often determines whether you eventually get the retainer or lose the prospect forever.

The Right Response Framework

Acknowledge and Validate

"Absolutely, this is an important decision and you should feel confident about it. I'd be concerned if you wanted to rush into something this significant."

Identify Specific Concerns

"What specific aspects do you want to think through? Maybe I can provide some additional information that would be helpful."

Offer Continued Support

"What questions can I answer to help you with that thinking process? I want to make sure you have everything you need to make the best decision."

Set Specific Follow-Up Timeline

"When would be a good time for us to reconnect? Tomorrow evening? Friday morning?" Don't leave it open-ended.

Provide Clear Guidance

"Regardless of your decision, here's what you should be doing in the meantime to protect yourself..."

What Not to Do

Don't pressure them to decide immediately. Don't assume they're not interested. Don't fail to follow up appropriately. Don't leave them without guidance for next steps.

COMMON CLOSING MISTAKES TO AVOID

Talking Past the Close

Continuing to sell after they've already decided to hire you is one of the most common and costly mistakes. When they say "Let's do this," stop talking about benefits and start getting their information.

Multiple Choice Overload

Giving them too many options creates confusion and decision paralysis. Keep choices simple and limited.

Apologizing for Your Investment

"I know it's a lot of money, but..." undermines all the value you've spent time building. Your fees are appropriate for the service you provide.

Rushing the Decision Process

Not allowing proper processing time makes them feel pressured and triggers resistance. Respect their need to think through important decisions.

Accepting "Maybe" as an Answer

"Maybe" isn't a decision. It's avoidance. Clarify what they need to move from maybe to yes or no.

PRACTICE SCENARIOS

The Eager Buyer

Prospect: "Yes, I want to hire you. What do we do next?"

Response: "Excellent. Let me get your retainer information handled right now, and then I'll walk you through exactly what happens next and what you can expect."

The Hesitant Buyer

Prospect: "I think I want to hire you, but I'm nervous about spending this much money."

Response: "That's completely understandable—this is a significant investment. What specifically are you most concerned about? Let's address that directly so you feel confident about moving forward."

The Price-Sensitive Buyer

Prospect: "This is more than I was hoping to spend. Do you have any payment options?"

Response: "I understand this is a substantial investment. Let me show you some flexible payment options we have available. But let's also talk about what's really at stake if this isn't handled properly, because that context is important for your decision."

The Multiple Decision Maker

Prospect: "I need to talk to my husband before I can commit to anything."

Response: "Absolutely—this affects your whole family. Would it be helpful if I spoke with both of you together so he can ask questions directly and feel comfortable with the decision?"

MEASURING CLOSING EFFECTIVENESS

Track these metrics to improve your closing skills:

Conversion Rate from Consultation to Retainer: What percentage of qualified prospects ultimately hire you?

Time from Initial Contact to Retainer: How long does your typical closing process take?

Objection Patterns: What concerns come up most frequently during closing conversations?

Follow-Up Success Rates: When prospects need time to think, how often do they return to hire you?

Payment Method Preferences: How do clients typically prefer to handle retainer payments?

CHAPTER SUMMARY

Closing criminal defense clients requires a fundamentally different approach than traditional sales closing. The consultative method works because it respects client psychology while guiding them toward the protection they need.

The three-question close framework—"What makes sense?" "What do you need to know?" "What happens next?"—puts decision ownership with the client while maintaining momentum toward hiring.

Creating urgency based on legitimate factors like court deadlines and evidence preservation is more effective than artificial pressure tactics that trigger defensive responses.

The strategic pricing pause allows prospects to mentally prepare for investment levels, reducing sticker shock and making fees seem more reasonable.

Recognizing buying signals and using strategic silence prevents talking past the close while giving prospects space to make decisions.

Handling "let me think about it" through validation, clarification, and structured follow-up maintains relationships with prospects who aren't ready to decide immediately.

When you've properly built rapport, demonstrated value, and addressed concerns throughout the intake process, closing becomes a natural conversation about moving forward rather than a high-pressure sales situation.

In the next chapter, we'll explore follow-up systems that actually work—how to stay connected with prospects who weren't ready to hire initially and convert them when circumstances change, while maintaining professionalism and avoiding the appearance of being pushy or desperate.

CHAPTER 8:

FOLLOW-UP SYSTEMS THAT WORK

Here's a painful truth that most attorneys refuse to acknowledge: they give up after the first "no" and lose 80% of their potential business. Someone calls, you have what feels like a great conversation, they say "I need to think about it," and you never follow up systematically. Three weeks later, they hire someone else.

This pattern is endemic in criminal defense practices across the country. Attorneys have excellent initial conversations, build rapport, demonstrate value, handle objections effectively, and then completely abandon prospects who aren't ready to make immediate hiring decisions.

The fundamental misunderstanding here is treating criminal defense like traditional sales. This isn't car sales or insurance sales where people are actively shopping and ready to buy. Your potential clients are dealing with arrest trauma, family stress, financial concerns, and complete unfamiliarity with the legal system. They're not going to make a hiring decision in ten minutes, no matter how skilled your intake conversation was.

The statistics reveal the real opportunity: it takes an average of seven touchpoints to convert a criminal defense prospect into a client. Most attorneys make two attempts and quit. But successful attorneys understand that proper follow-up isn't annoying when it's done correctly—it's helpful, professional, and demonstrates genuine concern for their situation.

This chapter will show you how to systematically convert prospects who weren't ready to hire you initially while maintaining professionalism and building long-term relationships that generate referrals for years.

THE PSYCHOLOGY OF FOLLOW-UP IN CRIMINAL DEFENSE

Understanding why criminal clients need multiple touchpoints is crucial for developing effective follow-up systems. Their decision-making process is fundamentally different from normal consumer behavior due to the trauma and complexity of their situation.

Why Criminal Clients Need Multiple Touchpoints

Emotional Processing Time Required After Arrest Trauma

Their brain is still in crisis mode for days or weeks after the arrest. The stress hormones, sleep disruption, and psychological shock of being arrested don't resolve quickly. They literally cannot make fully rational decisions immediately, regardless of how logical your presentation was.

Information Overwhelm During Crisis Creates Decision Paralysis

During your intake call, you provided comprehensive legal information when their brain was already overloaded. They need time to process and absorb what you told them, research options, and regain some sense of control over their situation.

Financial Stress and Family Consultation Requirements

They need to figure out how to pay for representation, discuss the situation with their spouse, possibly talk to family members about borrowing money, and coordinate their financial response to an unexpected major expense.

Comparison Shopping Despite Emotional Connection

Even after an excellent conversation with you, they might still call other attorneys to make sure they're making the right decision. This isn't necessarily about price—it's about gaining confidence through comparison.

Court Date Realities and Timeline Pressures

Sometimes they have weeks before their next court date, so there's no immediate pressure to decide. Other times they initially think they can handle the situation themselves, then realize they need professional help as the court date approaches.

The Follow-Up Advantage in Criminal Defense

Most Attorneys Quit After Two Attempts

You're competing against lawyers who give up quickly, which means consistent follow-up automatically differentiates you from most of your competition.

Consistent Follow-Up Demonstrates Commitment

It shows you actually care about their outcome, not just getting the retainer check. This builds trust and confidence in your genuine concern for their wellbeing.

Multiple Touchpoints Build Familiarity and Trust

Each interaction deepens the relationship and makes hiring you feel more natural and less risky from their perspective.

Timing-Based Conversions

Sometimes they're not ready to hire anyone in week one, but they desperately need an attorney by week three when reality sets in or their court date approaches.

THE 7-TOUCH AUTOMATED FOLLOW-UP SEQUENCE

This proven sequence converts prospects without being annoying by focusing on value delivery rather than sales pressure. Each touch serves a specific psychological purpose in building the relationship.

Touch 1: Immediate Post-Call Email (Within 1 Hour)

Purpose: Recap conversation and provide promised resources

Content Strategy: "Thank you for taking the time to speak with me today about your situation. As promised, I'm attaching our guide to Connecticut DUI procedures and the courthouse information for your specific location. I also wanted to recap the key points we discussed..."

Psychology: Shows you listen carefully and follow through on small promises, which builds confidence in your ability to follow through on bigger commitments.

Specific Elements to Include:
- Reference specific details from your conversation

- Provide promised resources immediately
- Summarize next steps and timeline
- Include direct contact information for questions

Touch 2: Educational Value Email (Day 3)

Purpose: Provide additional helpful information without selling

Content Strategy: "I was thinking about your situation and the concerns you mentioned about your job security. I wanted to share some additional information that might be helpful as you're figuring out your next steps..."

Psychology: Demonstrates ongoing concern and positions you as a resource rather than just a vendor seeking business.

Specific Elements to Include:
- Address specific concerns they mentioned
- Provide actionable information they can use regardless of who they hire
- Reference their timeline and decision-making process
- Avoid any direct sales language

Touch 3: Personal Check-In Call (Day 7)

Purpose: Genuine concern and availability confirmation

Content Strategy: "I wanted to check in and see how you're doing since we spoke last week. Have you had a chance to review the information I sent? Do you have any additional questions after having time to think about everything?"

Psychology: Personal touch builds relationship depth and shows you view them as a person, not just a potential client.

Conversation Guidelines:
- Keep it brief unless they want to talk longer
- Focus on their wellbeing and concerns
- Answer any questions that have come up
- Reconfirm your availability without pressure

Touch 4: Case Update Email (Day 14)

Purpose: Share relevant legal developments or similar case outcomes

Content Strategy: "I wanted to update you on a recent development in a similar case that might interest you. Last week, we had a favorable outcome for another client facing very similar charges..."

Psychology: Shows active engagement in their area of concern and demonstrates ongoing success with cases like theirs.

Content Guidelines:
- Maintain strict confidentiality while sharing general outcomes
- Focus on developments relevant to their specific situation
- Provide context for how this might affect their case
- Avoid making promises about their specific outcome

Touch 5: Final Direct Outreach (Day 21)

Purpose: Clear timeline and decision guidance

Content Strategy: "Your court date is approaching in two weeks, and I wanted to make sure you have everything you need to make the best decision for your situation. If you'd like to move forward with representation, we should get started this week to allow adequate preparation time."

Psychology: Creates appropriate urgency based on real deadlines rather than artificial pressure.

Key Messages:
- Reference approaching deadlines that matter for their case
- Offer specific timeline for getting started
- Maintain supportive tone rather than pressure
- Provide clear next steps if they're ready to proceed

Touch 6: Resource Sharing (Day 30)

Purpose: Continued value without direct sales pressure

Content Strategy: "I came across this article about employment implications of criminal charges and thought it might be relevant to your situation, especially given your concerns about your professional license."

Psychology: Demonstrates long-term thinking about their concerns and continued investment in their success.

Resource Selection:
- Choose resources directly relevant to their expressed concerns
- Focus on long-term implications they might not have considered
- Provide actionable information regardless of their attorney choice
- Maintain your expertise positioning through quality resource curation

Touch 7: Final Professional Contact (Day 45)

Purpose: Professional closure with future availability

Content Strategy: "I know you've probably made decisions about your representation by now. I hope everything is working out well for you. If circumstances change or you need guidance down the road, please don't hesitate to reach out."

Psychology: Leaves the door open without being pushy and demonstrates professional class and genuine concern for their wellbeing.

Closing Elements:
- Assume they've moved forward with someone else
- Express genuine hope for positive outcomes
- Leave door open for future contact
- Maintain professional dignity and respect

CONTENT STRATEGY FOR EACH TOUCH

The effectiveness of your follow-up system depends heavily on providing genuine value in each interaction rather than just asking for business repeatedly.

Educational Content That Builds Trust

Legal Process Explanations
Provide specific information about their charges, their courthouse, and what they can expect. This helps them feel more prepared and confident regardless of who they ultimately hire.

Rights Protection Information
Share information they can use immediately to protect themselves, such as what to say (or not say) if contacted by law enforcement, how to handle media inquiries, or what to do about social media during pending cases.

Consequence Minimization Strategies
Provide actionable steps they can take to minimize collateral consequences while their case is pending, such as voluntary counseling, community service, or professional development that might benefit their case.

Personal Touch Techniques

Reference Specific Conversation Details
"You mentioned being concerned about your job security..." or "I remember you were worried about telling your parents..." These references show you were truly listening and view them as an individual.

Acknowledge Their Decision-Making Process
"I know you wanted to discuss this with your family..." or "I understand you're taking time to explore all your options..." This respects their autonomy and timeline.

Provide Situation-Specific Updates
Share information about legal developments, similar cases, or courthouse changes that specifically affect their situation rather than generic legal news.

Value-Added Follow-Up Content

Courthouse-Specific Guidance
"Since your case is in Bridgeport Superior Court, here's what you should know about parking, security procedures, and what to expect when you arrive..."

Timeline Management
"With your court date three weeks away, here's what you should be thinking about and preparing for, regardless of whether you hire an attorney or represent yourself..."

Professional Consequences Information
"For someone in your profession, here are the specific licensing implications to consider and steps you can take to protect your career..."

Family Impact Guidance
"For parents, here's how to discuss this situation with children appropriately and protect them from unnecessary stress..."

AUTOMATION WITHOUT LOSING PERSONALIZATION

Technology should enable personal touch at scale, not replace human connection. The goal is to automate timing and structure while maintaining genuine personalization in every interaction.

Email Automation Best Practices

Template Foundation with Personal Customization
Start with proven templates that ensure consistent messaging and psychological effectiveness, but customize each message with specific details from their conversation and situation.

Calendar-Based Trigger System
Automate the timing based on the proven sequence, but don't automate the content. Each follow-up should feel personally crafted for their specific situation.

Response Monitoring and Human Intervention
When prospects respond to any automated follow-up, immediately switch to personal, human communication. Automated systems should facilitate human connection, not replace it.

CRM Integration for Comprehensive Tracking

Track every interaction, response, and personal detail for future reference. This enables truly personalized follow-up even months later.

Maintaining Personal Touch in Automated Systems

Conversation Detail Integration
Reference specific details from your original conversation in every follow-up message to demonstrate that you remember and care about their individual situation.

Unique Situation Acknowledgment
Acknowledge their specific concerns, timeline, and circumstances in each communication rather than using generic messages.

Relevant Timing Coordination
Provide information and guidance based on their actual court dates and case progression rather than arbitrary scheduling.

Direct Response Encouragement
Include direct contact information and encourage personal responses rather than automated replies. Make it easy for them to reach you when they're ready.

ADVANCED FOLLOW-UP STRATEGIES

Beyond the basic seven-touch sequence, sophisticated follow-up strategies can convert prospects who might not respond to standard approaches and build long-term relationships that generate referrals.

Holiday and Special Occasion Follow-Up

Birthday and Holiday Greetings

Send brief, personal greetings to prospects who had good conversations but didn't hire you. These maintain positive relationships without sales pressure.

Anniversary Acknowledgment

For prospects who had serious cases, a supportive check-in on the anniversary of their arrest can be meaningful and appreciated.

Professional Milestone Recognition

If you see LinkedIn updates or news about their career advancement, acknowledge their success. This builds goodwill and keeps you top-of-mind for referrals.

Referral-Based Re-Engagement

Similar Case Messaging

"I have a client in a similar situation" messages demonstrate ongoing work in their area and can prompt reconsideration of their representation needs.

Legal Update Communications

When laws change that affect their situation or case type, provide updates that demonstrate your ongoing expertise and concern for their area of legal needs.

Success Story Sharing

When you achieve favorable outcomes in similar cases, share appropriate success stories that might encourage them to reconsider their representation or refer others.

Long-Term Relationship Building

Quarterly Check-Ins

For prospects who had excellent conversations but timing wasn't right, quarterly check-ins can maintain relationships until circumstances change.

Educational Content Inclusion
Include interested prospects in your legal newsletter or educational content distribution (with permission) to maintain regular, valuable contact.

Speaking Event Invitations
When you present educational seminars or speak at events relevant to their situation, invite prospects who might benefit from the information.

MEASURING FOLLOW-UP SUCCESS

Systematic measurement allows you to optimize your follow-up approach and demonstrate ROI on the time and resources invested in prospect nurturing.

Key Performance Indicators

Response Rates by Touch
Track response rates to each message in the sequence to identify which approaches generate the most engagement and optimize accordingly.

Conversion Rates by Stage
Measure conversion rates at each stage of follow-up to understand which touches are most effective at moving prospects toward hiring decisions.

Time to Conversion Analysis

Track which touch typically produces the hire to optimize timing and identify the most effective conversion points in your sequence.

Referral Generation Tracking
Monitor referrals generated from follow-up contacts who don't hire but refer others, as this often represents significant long-term value.

Optimization Strategies

A/B Testing Implementation
Test different subject lines, messaging approaches, and content types to identify what resonates most effectively with your specific market.

Timing Optimization
Analyze response patterns and conversion data to optimize the timing of each touch for maximum effectiveness.

Content Refinement
Track which resources and information generate the most engagement and refine your content strategy accordingly.

Personalization Scaling
Develop systems to maintain quality personalization while increasing volume as your practice grows.

CHAPTER SUMMARY

Follow-up systems are crucial for criminal defense practices because prospects need time to process trauma, gather financial resources, and make important decisions about their representation. Most attorneys give up too quickly and lose substantial business to competitors who maintain systematic contact.

The seven-touch automated sequence provides value at each contact point while building relationships and maintaining top-of-mind awareness when prospects are ready to make hiring decisions.

Effective follow-up balances automation with personalization, using technology to manage timing and structure while maintaining genuine human connection and individual attention.

Advanced strategies including holiday follow-up, referral-based re-engagement, and long-term relationship building extend the value of prospect relationships beyond immediate conversions.

Systematic measurement and optimization ensure follow-up efforts generate maximum ROI while providing genuine value to prospects regardless of whether they ultimately hire your firm.

The attorneys who master follow-up systems convert twice as many prospects as those who rely solely on initial conversation closing. More importantly, they build referral networks and professional relationships that generate business for years while providing better service to people who need legal help during difficult times.

When implemented consistently, these follow-up systems transform prospects who weren't ready to hire initially into clients, referral sources, and long-term professional relationships that strengthen both your practice and your community's access to quality legal representation.

CHAPTER 9:

MEASURING AND IMPROVING YOUR INTAKE PERFORMANCE

What gets measured gets improved—but most attorneys measure the wrong things. They track conversion rates and think they understand their intake performance. They have no idea what's really happening in their practice.

Conversion rate alone doesn't tell you anything useful for improvement purposes. Was it a good month because you received better leads, or because your intake specialist improved their empathy skills? Did you lose clients because of price objections, or because someone on your team made inappropriate promises they couldn't keep? Without granular performance data, you're flying blind.

You can't improve what you can't measure, and you can't measure what you don't track systematically. Most criminal defense practices operate on gut feelings and assumptions rather than data-driven insights about what actually drives successful conversions.

This chapter will show you how to build a comprehensive intake performance optimization system that uses advanced analytics and AI technology to transform subjective communication skills into objective, measurable data that drives consistent improvement.

THE LIMITATIONS OF BASIC CONVERSION TRACKING

Most attorneys track only the most basic metrics: how many calls came in, how many people hired them, and what their conversion percentage was. This approach provides virtually no actionable information for improvement.

Why Conversion Rate Alone Is Misleading

Conversion rates fluctuate based on dozens of variables that have nothing to do with intake performance: lead quality, market conditions, seasonal factors, case mix, timing of calls, and external events affecting your target market.

A month with high conversion rates might reflect excellent lead quality rather than improved intake skills. A month with low conversion rates might reflect a new intake specialist learning the role rather than systemic problems with your approach.

Without understanding the underlying factors that drive conversion, you can't replicate success or address failure effectively.

The False Assumption of Uniform Lead Quality

Most practices assume all leads are created equal, but this assumption destroys the accuracy of performance analysis. A referral from another attorney has completely different conversion dynamics than a Google Ad click from someone shopping around.

When you mix different lead types together in conversion analysis, you lose the ability to understand what's actually working and what needs improvement.

The Problem with Lagging Indicators

Conversion rates are lagging indicators—they tell you what happened after it's too late to change it. They don't provide real-time feedback for improvement or early warning signs of developing problems.

Leading indicators like call quality metrics, client engagement levels, and satisfaction scores predict future conversion rates and allow for proactive improvement rather than reactive problem-solving.

KEY METRICS THAT ACTUALLY MATTER

Effective intake performance measurement requires a comprehensive funnel analysis that tracks leading indicators, process metrics, and quality factors that drive long-term success.

Lead Quality and Source Performance Metrics

Lead Source Conversion Rates by Channel

Google ads might convert at 15% while referrals convert at 45%. Understanding these differences allows you to optimize marketing spend and set realistic expectations for different lead types.

Time from Initial Inquiry to First Contact

Speed matters incredibly in criminal defense. Leads contacted within one hour convert at significantly higher rates than leads contacted after 24 hours. This metric identifies responsiveness problems that kill conversions.

Qualified vs. Unqualified Lead Ratio

If you're receiving many calls but achieving low conversion rates, you might have a lead quality problem rather than an intake performance issue. This metric helps distinguish between marketing problems and sales problems.

Geographic Distribution Analysis

Which areas of your market are most profitable? Where should you focus advertising spend? Geographic analysis reveals market opportunities and helps optimize resource allocation.

Lead Value Assessment and Lifetime Client Worth Prediction

Not all leads are equal in potential value. DUI leads might convert at 20% but be worth $5,000 each. Assault leads might convert at 10% but be worth $15,000 each. Understanding lead value helps prioritize follow-up efforts and resource allocation.

Process and Performance Metrics

Average Call Duration by Outcome

Successful conversions usually require longer conversations to build rapport and address concerns. If your average call duration is under 15 minutes, you're probably not building sufficient trust and connection.

Number of Touchpoints Required for Conversion by Lead Source

Google leads might convert on the first call due to urgency, but referrals might need multiple touchpoints because they're less urgency-driven. Understanding these patterns helps optimize follow-up strategies.

Time from First Contact to Signed Retainer

This metric reveals the effectiveness of your follow-up processes and closing skills. Long cycles might indicate indecisive prospects or ineffective nurturing systems.

Follow-Up Sequence Completion Rates

Are prospects engaging with your automated sequences? Which messages get the best response rates? This data helps optimize your follow-up content and timing.

Team Member Performance Consistency

Are all your intake specialists performing equally, or do you have training and development opportunities? Individual performance tracking identifies coaching needs and best practices to replicate.

Outcome and Financial Metrics

Overall Conversion Rate Segmented by Intake Specialist

Who's your best performer? What are they doing differently? Individual performance analysis reveals coaching opportunities and successful techniques to teach others.

Average Case Value by Intake Method

Do phone intakes produce higher-value cases than web form inquiries? Understanding these patterns helps optimize intake channel investment and staffing.

Client Satisfaction Scores Specific to Intake Experience

Happy clients refer more prospects and leave better reviews. Intake satisfaction directly impacts long-term business development through word-of-mouth marketing.

Referral Generation Rates from Positive Intake Experiences

Great intake experiences create natural word-of-mouth marketing. Tracking referral generation from satisfied prospects (even those who don't hire you) reveals the long-term value of quality intake processes.

Quality Metrics (Most Important for Long-Term Success)

This category is where most attorneys completely miss the mark. They focus on conversion rates instead of quality indicators that predict sustainable success.

Empathy Demonstration Score Using Standardized Criteria

Are your intake specialists actually connecting with clients emotionally? Empathy can be measured through language pattern analysis and client feedback, and it's the strongest predictor of conversion success.

Question-Answering Completeness and Accuracy

Are specialists providing thorough, helpful responses to client concerns? Incomplete or inaccurate information damages trust and reduces conversion probability.

Professional Presentation Rating

Do specialists sound organized, knowledgeable, and trustworthy? Professional presentation affects both immediate conversion and long-term referral generation.

Client Comfort Level and Trust-Building Effectiveness

This metric measures what actually drives hiring decisions. Clients hire attorneys they trust, not necessarily the most qualified attorneys. Trust-building effectiveness is measurable and improvable.

AI-ENHANCED INTAKE PERFORMANCE ANALYSIS

Advanced artificial intelligence systems can now analyze intake calls objectively and provide specific feedback on subjective communication skills. This technology transforms qualitative performance into quantitative data.

The Complete 10-Point AI Scoring System

This comprehensive scoring system analyzes every intake call on ten specific criteria, providing objective data about subjective performance with a total possible score of 100 points:

Rapport Building (15 points)
AI measures empathy markers, voice tone patterns, and connection-building language. It can detect when someone is genuinely building rapport versus going through the motions mechanically.

Case Handling Confirmation (10 points)

AI detects whether the specialist clearly communicated your firm's capability to handle their specific case type and addressed their particular concerns about representation.

Empathy Display (15 points)
Language pattern analysis for emotional connection. The AI looks for validation phrases, emotional acknowledgment, and supportive language that creates psychological safety.

Question Responsiveness (15 points)
AI tracks whether every client question received a complete and thorough response, or if concerns were missed, dismissed, or inadequately addressed.

Time Distribution Balance (10 points)
Speaking time ratio analysis. Successful intake calls have proper balance—too much talking from the specialist kills rapport and prevents trust building.

Special Concerns Identification (10 points)
AI recognizes whether the specialist identified and addressed client-specific priorities beyond the obvious legal issues, such as employment, family, or professional licensing concerns.

Financial Discussion Management (10 points)
AI assesses how value was communicated before price, and whether the investment was positioned appropriately within the context of consequences and protection.

Presumptive Language Avoidance (5 points)
AI detection of pushy or presumptive language that destroys trust with criminal clients who are already feeling vulnerable and defensive.

Promises Made Management (5 points)

AI flagging of inappropriate commitments or guarantees that could create ethical problems or unrealistic expectations that damage client relationships.

Knowledge Gaps Identification (5 points)
AI recognition of areas where the specialist needed more training or information to effectively address client concerns and questions.

AI Implementation Strategy

Weekly Call Review Sessions
AI analysis combined with team discussion of patterns and improvement opportunities. This creates a culture of continuous learning based on objective data rather than subjective impressions.

Monthly Performance Evaluations
Comprehensive scoring and individual improvement planning using AI-identified strengths and weaknesses. This enables targeted coaching rather than generic training.

Quarterly Team Assessments
Overall performance review and goal setting with AI-driven insights about team trends, successful patterns, and areas needing systematic improvement.

Technology Integration Requirements

Implementing AI-enhanced performance analysis requires specific technology infrastructure:

Call Recording with Legal Compliance
Proper consent procedures and secure storage systems that comply with attorney-client privilege and confidentiality requirements.

AI Transcription and Analysis Platform Integration
Systems that can accurately transcribe legal conversations and analyze communication patterns for the specific criteria that matter in criminal defense intake.

Automated Scoring Algorithms
Technology that can consistently apply scoring criteria across hundreds of calls to provide objective performance measurement.

Performance Tracking Dashboards
Visual reporting systems that make performance data accessible and actionable for both individual specialists and practice managers.

Individual Improvement Plan Development Tools
Systems that translate AI analysis into specific coaching recommendations and training priorities for each team member.

BUILDING A CULTURE OF CONTINUOUS IMPROVEMENT

Technology is only as effective as the culture that uses it. Creating an environment where improvement is expected, celebrated, and systematically supported is crucial for long-term success.

Team Development and Growth Approach

Regular Training and Coaching Sessions
Weekly skill building based on AI performance data rather than generic training programs. This targeted approach addresses specific weaknesses identified through objective analysis.

Peer Review and Learning Opportunities

Team members learning from each other's successful calls identified through AI analysis. The best-performing calls become training materials that demonstrate proven techniques.

Success Story Analysis
Understanding what works and why it works, validated by AI analysis of hundreds of calls rather than subjective impressions or isolated examples.

Challenge Identification and Solution Development
Collaborative problem-solving based on data patterns rather than guesswork or assumptions about what might be causing conversion problems.

Performance Management and Accountability

Individual Improvement Plans
Customized development based on AI analysis of specific performance gaps. If someone scores low on empathy, they receive targeted empathy training rather than generic communication coaching.

Team-Wide Best Practice Sharing
Cross-pollination of successful techniques identified through AI pattern recognition across multiple high-performing specialists.

Recognition and Reward Systems
Celebrating excellence and improvement using data-driven metrics that reward genuine skill development rather than arbitrary favorites.

System Evolution and Optimization

Regular Script and Process Updates
Continuous refinement based on AI-identified successful patterns and language that consistently produces better outcomes.

Technology Upgrades and Integration
Staying current with advancing AI capabilities and integrating new tools that provide additional insights into performance improvement.

Market Feedback Incorporation
Client input and market response data driving system improvements to ensure continued relevance and effectiveness.

ADVANCED AI APPLICATIONS IN INTAKE OPTIMIZATION

Beyond basic performance scoring, advanced AI applications can provide real-time coaching and predictive analytics that transform intake effectiveness.

Real-Time Coaching and Feedback

Live Performance Guidance
AI providing real-time feedback during calls with prompts like "Client mentioned job concerns—address professional licensing impact" or "Client seems overwhelmed—slow down and provide reassurance."

Dynamic Script Adaptation
AI customizing conversation approaches based on client responses and behavioral patterns detected during the call.

Immediate Correction Opportunities
AI identifying missed opportunities or problematic language in real-time, allowing specialists to adjust their approach within the same conversation.

Predictive Analytics and Optimization

Conversion Probability Forecasting
AI predicting conversion likelihood based on early call indicators, allowing you to focus follow-up resources on the most promising prospects.

Optimal Timing Recommendations
AI suggesting the best times to contact specific prospects based on their behavioral patterns and response history.

Personalization Optimization
AI customizing approach recommendations based on client type, case type, and individual psychological indicators detected through communication patterns.

Pattern Recognition and Trend Analysis

Cross-Call Pattern Identification
AI identifying successful patterns across hundreds of calls that human analysis would miss, such as specific phrase combinations that consistently improve conversion rates.

Market Trend Integration
AI correlating intake performance with external market factors to optimize messaging and approach based on current conditions.

Competitive Intelligence

AI analysis of what works best against specific types of competition or in particular market segments.

IMPLEMENTATION ROADMAP FOR AI-ENHANCED INTAKE

Month 1: Foundation Setup
- Basic AI grading system installation and configuration
- Team training on scoring criteria and improvement methodology
- Initial baseline performance measurement
- Technology integration and workflow optimization

Month 2: Advanced Analytics Integration
- Comprehensive reporting dashboard implementation
- Historical data analysis to identify trends and patterns
- Individual performance assessment and goal setting
- Advanced training program development based on AI insights

Month 3: Real-Time Coaching Implementation
- Live feedback system activation and specialist training
- Process optimization based on initial AI recommendations
- Advanced scoring methodology refinement
- Team performance comparison and best practice identification

Month 4: Predictive Modeling and Optimization
- Conversion prediction algorithm implementation
- Advanced personalization feature activation
- Market correlation analysis and strategic optimization
- Comprehensive system evaluation and future planning

MONTHLY AND QUARTERLY REVIEW PROCESSES

Monthly Review Process

Performance Data Collection and Analysis
Comprehensive metrics gathering using AI-generated reports that provide both individual and team-wide insights into performance trends and improvement opportunities.

Team Feedback and Discussion Sessions
Collaborative improvement planning based on actual performance data rather than subjective opinions or assumptions about what might be working or failing.

Improvement Initiative Planning and Implementation
Specific action steps and accountability measures based on identified weaknesses and opportunities revealed through systematic analysis.

Quarterly Assessment and Strategic Planning

Comprehensive System Evaluation
Complete performance review with AI trend analysis that reveals long-term patterns and strategic opportunities for practice growth and improvement.

Client Feedback Integration and Analysis
External perspective validation of internal performance metrics through systematic client satisfaction surveys and feedback analysis.

Market Condition Adjustments and Optimization
Adapting strategies and approaches based on changing competitive environment and market conditions revealed through performance data.

Annual Planning and Goal Setting

Performance Target Establishment
Setting realistic but challenging goals based on historical performance data and AI projections rather than arbitrary targets or wishful thinking.

Technology Roadmap Development
Planning for continued advancement in AI capabilities and integration opportunities that will further improve intake performance and practice efficiency.

Team Development and Career Planning
Individual career growth planning based on performance strengths and development opportunities identified through comprehensive AI analysis.

CHAPTER SUMMARY

Measuring and improving intake performance requires moving beyond simple conversion rate tracking to comprehensive analysis of leading indicators, process metrics, and quality factors that drive long-term success.

AI-enhanced performance analysis transforms subjective communication skills into objective, measurable data that enables targeted improvement rather than generic training approaches.

The 10-point AI scoring system provides comprehensive evaluation of rapport building, empathy display, question responsiveness, and other critical factors that determine conversion success.

Building a culture of continuous improvement based on data rather than opinions creates sustainable performance enhancement that benefits both the practice and the clients it serves.

Advanced AI applications including real-time coaching, predictive analytics, and pattern recognition provide sophisticated optimization opportunities that go far beyond basic performance measurement.

Systematic implementation of AI-enhanced performance measurement, combined with structured review processes and targeted improvement initiatives, creates predictable and sustainable growth in intake effectiveness.

When intake performance becomes measurable and improvable through systematic data analysis, practices can achieve consistent conversion rate improvements while providing better service to people who need legal representation during difficult times.

In the next chapter, we'll explore how to train non-lawyer team members to handle intake calls effectively and ethically, expanding your intake capacity while maintaining quality and compliance with professional responsibility requirements.

CHAPTER 10:

NON-LAWYER INTAKE SPECIALISTS & ASSOCIATES WHO SELL

Every successful criminal defense firm faces the same scalability bottleneck: as you grow, you can't personally handle every intake call. But the moment you hand off intake responsibilities to someone else, your conversion rates often plummet dramatically.

I learned this lesson the hard way during Ruane Attorneys' growth phase. For the first ten years, I handled every single intake call myself. My conversion rates were strong, but I was completely trapped. I couldn't take vacations, couldn't focus on high-level strategy, and couldn't scale the business because everything depended on my personal availability around the clock.

When I finally attempted to delegate intake responsibilities, disaster struck. My conversion rates dropped by nearly 40%. I was losing potential clients constantly because my team didn't understand the psychology of criminal clients, didn't have the right financial incentives to convert leads, and frankly, didn't have sufficient legal knowledge to handle complex questions that arose during intake conversations.

This chapter will show you how to build an intake team that maintains conversion rates while providing the scalability you need to grow your practice. You'll learn the ethical framework for what non-lawyers can and cannot do, why associates should never handle intake, and how to create compensation structures that align personal success with business success.

THE LEGAL AND ETHICAL FRAMEWORK FOR NON-LAWYER INTAKE

Before discussing tactics and techniques, we must address compliance with professional responsibility rules. Unauthorized practice of law violations can result in disciplinary action and destroy your professional reputation.

What Non-Lawyers CAN Do Legally and Ethically

Information Gathering and Administrative Tasks

Non-lawyer staff can collect basic case information, contact details, and background information necessary for attorney evaluation. They can schedule appointments, consultations, and coordinate court appearance logistics. They're permitted to explain firm policies, procedures, and general business practices, and discuss general fee structures, payment options, and administrative processes.

Educational Information and Resource Sharing

Staff members can explain general legal processes and typical procedures that are matters of public knowledge. They can share publicly available legal information and resources, describe what typically happens in similar case types, and provide firm marketing materials, brochures, and educational content.

Client Coordination and Support Services

Non-lawyers can coordinate between clients and attorneys, manage scheduling and communications, provide general information about court procedures and requirements, and assist with administrative aspects of representation.

What Non-Lawyers CANNOT Do (Critical Legal Boundaries)

Legal Advice Prohibition

Non-lawyer staff cannot provide advice on legal strategy, tactics, or case-specific approaches. They cannot interpret laws, statutes, court rules, or legal precedents. They're prohibited from predicting case outcomes or providing legal opinions, and cannot recommend specific legal actions or strategic decisions.

Attorney Work Product and Representation

Staff members cannot draft legal documents, motions, or formal legal correspondence. They cannot negotiate with prosecutors, judges, or opposing counsel. They cannot make court appearances or represent clients in any legal proceedings, and cannot sign legal correspondence or documents on behalf of the firm.

Client Confidentiality and Professional Responsibility

All non-lawyer staff must be trained on attorney-client privilege requirements and confidentiality obligations. They must understand the boundaries of their authority and when to immediately transfer calls to attorneys.

Connecticut-Specific Ethical Considerations

Rule 5.3 - Responsibilities Regarding Nonlawyer Assistants

This rule establishes attorney supervision requirements and accountability standards. It mandates specific training and competence standards for non-lawyer staff and requires compliance with client confidentiality obligations and information protection protocols.

Rule 5.5 - Unauthorized Practice of Law Prevention

This rule defines clear activity boundaries and limitation definitions for non-lawyer staff. It requires supervision documentation and oversight procedures, and mandates client disclosure requirements about non-lawyer status during initial contacts.

Compliance Script Examples

Train your staff to use these specific phrases when approaching legal boundaries:

"That's an excellent legal question that I'll need to have Attorney Ruane address with you directly."

"Let me connect you with one of our attorneys to discuss case strategy—that's their area of expertise."

"I can explain our general process, but the attorney will provide specific advice for your situation."

"That requires legal analysis, so let me get you connected with the right attorney immediately."

TRAINING NON-LAWYERS TO BUILD CREDIBILITY WITHOUT PRACTICING LAW

The key to successful non-lawyer intake is positioning staff members as professional coordinators rather than legal advisors while building credibility through process expertise.

The "Legal Coordinator" Professional Positioning

Transform Their Identity and Role

Instead of positioning staff as "just the intake person who answers phones," train them to say: "I'm your legal coordinator— I ensure you get connected with the right resources and attorney for your situation."

Instead of allowing them to say "I don't know anything about legal matters," teach them to position themselves as: "I specialize in helping clients navigate our process and connect with our legal team effectively."

Building Credibility Through Process and System Expertise

System Knowledge Demonstration

"Here's exactly what happens next in cases like yours, and I'll make sure you're prepared for each step."

This approach builds confidence without providing legal advice. They're explaining process, not predicting outcomes or recommending strategy.

Resource Awareness Display

"Let me connect you with Attorney Smith, who specializes specifically in these types of cases."

This demonstrates knowledge of your firm's capabilities and expertise without the staff member providing legal analysis.

Process Confidence Projection

"I've helped hundreds of clients through this exact situation, and I know exactly how to get you the support you need."

This builds confidence in their coordinating abilities without suggesting they provide legal guidance.

Professional Competence Communication

"Based on what you've shared, here's what our legal team will need to review to give you the best advice."

This shows they understand legal requirements without actually providing legal analysis.

The Authority Transfer Technique for Seamless Handoffs

Positioning Statement

"I work directly with our criminal defense attorneys to ensure every client receives exactly what they need for their specific situation."

Expertise Bridge

"Let me share what our attorneys typically see in situations similar to yours, and then connect you directly with them for specific guidance."

Professional Handoff

"I'm going to connect you with Attorney Johnson, who specializes in exactly these types of cases and will give you the specific legal guidance you need."

Training Scripts for Common Legal Boundary Situations

When Asked for Legal Advice

"That's exactly the type of question our attorneys are experts at answering. Let me make sure you're connected with Attorney Brown who handles cases like yours. In the meantime, I can explain our process and what information we'll need to get started."

When Discussing Case Strategy

"Our attorneys will develop the specific strategy for your case once they review all the details. What I can tell you is how our process works and what you can expect at each step."

When Asked to Predict Outcomes

"Every case is unique, and our attorneys will give you their honest assessment based on your specific facts. What I can share is how we've helped other clients in similar situations navigate this process successfully."

COMPENSATION STRUCTURES THAT INCENTIVIZE CONVERSION

Creating the right financial incentives is crucial for intake success. People perform best when their personal success aligns with business success.

Base Plus Performance Model (Recommended Structure)

Base Salary Component

Provides financial security and reduces desperation pressure that destroys rapport with prospects. Desperate people cannot build authentic relationships with clients in crisis.

Performance Bonus Structure

Rewards both conversion and quality metrics—not just closing deals, but closing them well. This prevents aggressive tactics that might convert short-term but damage long-term reputation.

Retention Component

Incentivizes long-term client relationships and satisfaction rather than just initial conversion. This creates accountability for the quality of the intake experience.

Example Compensation Structure

Base Annual Salary: $45,000-$55,000 (market competitive for your area)

Conversion Bonus: $25-$50 per successfully retained client

Quality Bonus: Additional $25 for intake scores consistently above 85 using objective scoring criteria

Quarterly Team Bonus: $200-$500 based on overall team performance metrics including client satisfaction and retention

Legal Considerations for Compensation Structure

Rule 5.4 Professional Independence Compliance

Fee splitting restrictions limit how you can structure bonuses. You can pay bonuses for conversion, but not percentages of legal fees collected from clients.

Client Cost Impact Considerations

Ensure that intake specialist compensation doesn't inappropriately inflate client costs or create conflicts of interest.

Documentation and Transparency Requirements

Maintain clear policies and procedures that comply with ethical rules and can withstand regulatory scrutiny.

WHY ASSOCIATES SHOULD NOT HANDLE INTAKE

This principle goes against conventional wisdom, but it's crucial for both ethical and practical reasons.

The Financial Incentive Problem with Associates

No Upside for Conversion Success

Associates receive the same salary regardless of intake results. They have zero personal financial motivation to convert leads effectively.

Perverse Incentive Effects

More successful intake means more work for the same pay. Unconsciously, associates may actually prefer fewer clients to reduce their workload.

Lack of Decision-Making Authority

Associates cannot make real-time pricing or service adjustments to close deals, eliminating flexibility that's often necessary for conversion.

Unconscious Sabotage Potential

They may discourage difficult or time-intensive cases to protect their workload, even if these cases would be profitable for the firm.

The Three Right Approaches for Intake

Option 1: Business Owner Handles All Sales (Highest Conversion)

- Maximum financial incentive to convert every viable lead
- Deepest understanding of firm value proposition and differentiation
- Authority to make real-time pricing and service adjustments
- Best positioned to build rapport with serious prospects
- Can pivot strategy mid-conversation based on client needs

Option 2: Dedicated Sales Attorney

- Hired specifically for business development and conversion
- Compensation directly tied to intake conversion metrics
- Legal knowledge to handle complex case discussions
- Full authority to close deals and make pricing decisions
- Focused solely on revenue generation, not case work

Option 3: Trained Non-Lawyer Salesperson with Proper Incentives

- Commission or bonus structure tied to successful conversions
- Trained extensively in your specific intake methodology
- Dedicated focus on conversion without case work distractions
- Can escalate complex legal questions to attorneys when needed
- Measured and rewarded based on conversion success

The Bottom Line on Motivation

Never put someone in charge of revenue generation who doesn't personally benefit from revenue generation. Human motivation is predictable—people perform best when their personal success aligns with business success.

MANAGING THE HANDOFF BETWEEN INTAKE SPECIALIST AND ATTORNEY

The transition from intake specialist to attorney is a critical moment that can either strengthen or undermine the client relationship.

Seamless Transition Protocol

Comprehensive Intake Summary

Specialist prepares detailed client information summary with everything the attorney needs to know about the prospect's situation, concerns, and priorities.

Question Documentation

All client concerns, questions, and priorities clearly noted so nothing gets missed during the attorney conversation.

Timeline and Urgency Information

Court dates, deadlines, and time-sensitive factors highlighted for immediate attorney attention and proper case management.

Expectation Setting

Client knows exactly what to expect from the attorney conversation, reducing anxiety and improving satisfaction.

Follow-Up Plan Coordination

Clear next steps communicated to both client and attorney to ensure continuity and professionalism.

Handoff Communication Scripts

From Specialist to Client

"I've gathered all your information and shared it with Attorney Johnson. They'll be calling you within 24 hours to discuss your legal options in detail. Here's what you can expect from that conversation..."

From Specialist to Attorney

"Client briefing for John Smith: DUI arrest last Friday, first offense, main concerns about job impact and professional license, court date next Tuesday, budget discussed at $5,000 range, specific questions about plea options and timeline."

IMPLEMENTATION STRATEGY AND TIMELINE

Month 1: Foundation Building

- Hire and begin comprehensive training of intake specialist on your methodology, legal boundaries, and compensation structure
- Establish clear protocols for legal compliance and supervision
- Implement tracking systems for performance measurement

Month 2: Supervised Practice Period

- Supervised practice period with coaching, system integration, and performance monitoring
- Ongoing legal compliance training and boundary reinforcement
- Client feedback collection and analysis

Month 3: Independent Operation

- Independent operation with ongoing coaching support, feedback, and performance optimization
- Advanced training based on initial performance patterns
- System refinement and process improvement

Month 4: Performance Evaluation

- Comprehensive performance evaluation, system optimization, and advanced training based on results

- Planning for potential team expansion based on success metrics
- Long-term strategy development for scalable growth

Success Metrics and Measurement

Conversion Rate Maintenance

Conversion rates should maintain or improve over the previous attorney-only model, demonstrating that delegation doesn't sacrifice effectiveness.

Client Satisfaction Scores

Client feedback about intake experience should remain high, indicating that non-lawyer staff can provide quality service.

Attorney Time Savings

Attorneys should have increased availability for higher-value activities like case work and court appearances.

Call Volume Capacity

Increased capacity to handle higher call volumes demonstrates scalability achievement.

Common Implementation Challenges

Client Resistance

Some clients prefer speaking directly with attorneys initially. Train your team to handle this professionally by explaining the process and emphasizing that they will speak with an attorney after initial coordination.

Quality Consistency

Maintaining standards across multiple team members requires systematic training, monitoring, and ongoing coaching.

Legal Compliance

Ongoing monitoring and training for ethical boundaries is non-negotiable and requires constant attention and reinforcement.

Performance Management

Balancing quality with conversion goals requires the right metrics, incentives, and management oversight.

CHAPTER SUMMARY

Building a successful non-lawyer intake team requires understanding legal boundaries, creating proper incentives, and implementing systematic training and management processes.

Non-lawyer staff can handle information gathering, administrative tasks, and educational information sharing, but cannot provide legal advice, predict outcomes, or engage in attorney work product.

Professional positioning as "legal coordinators" rather than "intake staff" builds credibility through process expertise rather than legal knowledge.

Associates should not handle intake due to misaligned incentives and lack of decision-making authority that kills conversion rates.

Proper compensation structures that reward both conversion and quality create the right motivation for sustainable success.

Seamless handoffs between intake specialists and attorneys ensure continuity and maintain client confidence throughout the process.

Systematic implementation with proper training, supervision, and performance measurement creates scalable growth without sacrificing conversion effectiveness.

When built correctly, non-lawyer intake teams provide the scalability needed for practice growth while maintaining the conversion rates essential for business success.

In the next chapter, we'll explore advanced techniques for handling difficult intake scenarios professionally, including angry callers, unrealistic clients, and challenging situations that test your systems and training.

CHAPTER 11:

TRAINING YOUR INTAKE TEAM

The ultimate challenge every successful criminal defense firm faces is building an intake team that converts at the same level you do personally. It's one thing to master intake yourself through years of experience and refinement. It's an entirely different challenge to systematically transfer that ability to other people who lack your experience, legal knowledge, and personal investment in the business.

Most attorneys assume they can simply hand someone a script and expect professional-level results. Six months later, their conversion rates have dropped 30%, client satisfaction has declined, and they can't understand why their carefully developed intake system isn't working when executed by others.

The problem isn't the script or the system—it's the absence of systematic people development. Converting prospects requires a complex combination of emotional intelligence, communication skills, product knowledge, and psychological awareness that must be developed through structured training and ongoing coaching.

The scalability challenge is real: maintaining quality while growing capacity. You can't be on every call forever, but you also can't afford to lose clients because your team isn't properly prepared to represent your firm effectively during these crucial first interactions.

This chapter will show you how to build intake team capacity systematically while maintaining the conversion rates and client satisfaction that drive practice growth.

HIRING FOR INTAKE SUCCESS

The foundation of effective intake team training is hiring people with the right characteristics and potential for development. You cannot train someone to genuinely care about people in crisis, but you can teach someone who already cares to do it more effectively.

Essential Characteristics and Personality Traits

High Emotional Intelligence (Non-Negotiable)

This characteristic predicts intake success more than any other factor. Prospects need to feel understood and supported during one of the most stressful experiences of their lives. Emotional intelligence cannot be taught—it must be present naturally and developed through training.

Look for candidates who naturally read and respond appropriately to emotions, who show genuine empathy in their interactions, and who can maintain emotional stability when dealing with stressed, angry, or upset people.

Authentic Active Listening Skills

Distinguish between people who are genuinely interested in helping others solve problems and those who are simply good at pretending to listen. Criminal clients are hypersensitive to authenticity, and they will detect insincerity immediately.

During interviews, assess whether candidates ask follow-up questions, remember details from earlier in conversations, and demonstrate genuine curiosity about other people's situations and concerns.

Stress Management and Resilience

Criminal intake involves dealing with people in crisis situations daily. Team members need the ability to remain calm, effective, and empathetic under pressure consistently, not just during their best moments.

Evaluate candidates' ability to handle multiple stressful situations simultaneously, their recovery time from difficult interactions, and their strategies for maintaining professional effectiveness during challenging periods.

Professional Communication Excellence

Since most clients will never meet your intake team in person, voice quality and phone presence are crucial. Team members must project confidence, competence, and warmth through their voice alone.

Assess clarity of speech, warmth of tone, professional vocabulary, and ability to adjust communication style appropriately for different types of callers.

Coachability and Growth Orientation

Intake skills require continuous refinement based on feedback, market changes, and performance analysis. Team members must be willing to learn, improve, and accept constructive feedback without defensiveness.

Look for candidates who ask questions about improvement opportunities, who seek feedback proactively, and who can implement suggestions effectively.

Comprehensive Interview Process Design

Initial Phone Screening Assessment

Before candidates ever visit your office, assess their voice quality, communication style, and phone presence through a structured phone interview. If they cannot handle a professional phone conversation during an interview, they cannot effectively represent your firm to prospects.

Live Role-Play Scenarios

Conduct real-world intake simulation exercises using actual difficult scenarios your team encounters regularly. Don't just ask hypothetical questions—require candidates to demonstrate the skills they claim to possess.

Stress Testing Under Pressure

Simulate difficult caller situations and assess emotional regulation capabilities. Can they remain professional, empathetic, and effective when someone is angry, unreasonable, or abusive?

Values Alignment Assessment

Evaluate candidates' client service philosophy and personal motivation for helping people in crisis. Understanding their "why" predicts long-term success better than technical skills.

Reference Verification with Focus

Contact previous supervisors specifically about candidates' coachability, improvement trajectory, and ability to handle feedback constructively. Past performance in learning and development predicts future training success.

Background and Experience Preferences

Customer Service Experience

Prefer candidates with foundation experience in client-facing problem-solving roles. They need to understand instinctively that their job is solving problems and helping people, not just processing calls efficiently.

Consultative Sales Experience

Sales experience can be valuable if it's consultative rather than pushy or manipulative. You want someone who can guide decisions through education and trust-building, not pressure tactics.

Crisis Intervention Experience

Experience in police dispatch, crisis hotlines, emergency room support, or similar high-stress helping roles provides excellent preparation for criminal defense intake.

Legal Background

Legal knowledge is helpful for context but not required if the foundational characteristics are strong. You can teach someone legal concepts, but you cannot teach them to genuinely care about people in crisis.

THE FOUR-WEEK SYSTEMATIC ONBOARDING PROCESS

Effective intake team development requires structured onboarding that builds skills systematically while integrating new team members into your firm culture and values.

Week 1: Foundation Building and Culture Immersion

Legal Ethics and Compliance Training

Begin with clear boundaries regarding unauthorized practice of law, confidentiality obligations, and ethical requirements. Team members must understand what they cannot do before learning what they can do.

Cover specific scenarios they'll encounter and provide exact language for transferring legal questions to attorneys appropriately.

Firm Values and Culture Integration

Immerse new team members in your core values and help them understand how these values translate into daily interactions with prospects and clients.

Connect their role to your firm's mission and help them understand how intake excellence serves justice by ensuring people get quality representation.

Basic Criminal Law Education

Provide context about charges, legal processes, and common client concerns without crossing into legal advice territory. They need enough knowledge to understand what clients are experiencing and what your attorneys do to help.

System and Technology Mastery

Train thoroughly on CRM systems, phone systems, scheduling tools, and communication platforms. Technology should enhance relationship building, not interfere with it.

Week 2: Skill Development and Technique Mastery

B.U.I.L.D. System Complete Integration

Train every element of the B.U.I.L.D. system until it becomes natural and comfortable rather than mechanical. They need to understand the psychology behind each component, not just memorize steps.

Empathy and Rapport Building Practice

Conduct extensive role-playing with immediate feedback and refinement. This is where most intake specialists struggle initially — make them practice until empathetic responses become automatic.

Objection Handling Comprehensive Training

Cover all three major objections with multiple variations and practice responses until they're comfortable addressing resistance without becoming defensive or pushy.

Follow-Up System Implementation

Teach the complete client journey from initial call through retention, including automated systems and personal touchpoint coordination.

Week 3: Supervised Practice and Real-World Application

Live Call Monitoring and Coaching

Allow new team members to handle real client interactions while you listen and provide immediate feedback. This bridges the gap between role-playing and independent performance.

Script Customization and Personal Adaptation

Help them adapt systematic frameworks to their individual communication style so responses feel natural rather than robotic.

Difficult Scenario Practice and Confidence Building

Expose them to challenging situations with support and guidance available. Build their confidence before they encounter difficult situations independently.

Performance Feedback Integration

Focus on specific improvement areas while recognizing strengths. Positive reinforcement combined with targeted development creates optimal learning conditions.

Week 4: Independence and Comprehensive Evaluation

Unsupervised Call Handling

Allow independent client interaction while ensuring support remains available when needed. Gradual independence builds confidence while maintaining quality.

Performance Metric Establishment

Set clear individual goals and measurement criteria so they understand exactly what success looks like in their role.

Ongoing Coaching Needs Assessment

Identify long-term development priorities and create six-month growth plans that align individual development with firm needs.

Full Team Integration

Complete their integration into team dynamics, support systems, and collaborative processes that sustain long-term performance.

MAINTAINING CONSISTENCY ACROSS MULTIPLE STAFF MEMBERS

As your intake team grows, maintaining quality and consistency becomes increasingly challenging. The goal is standardization without robotic uniformity.

Standardization Without Destroying Individuality

Core Framework with Personal Flexibility

Maintain non-negotiable psychological principles while allowing individual personality to emerge naturally. The structure stays consistent, but the specific words and style can vary.

Consistent Messaging with Individual Expression

Ensure every team member hits the same psychological triggers and covers essential information, but allow them to do so in their authentic voice.

Standard Processes with Adaptive Implementation

Keep the steps consistent while allowing execution to adapt to individual communication styles and specific client needs.

Quality Assurance Systems and Monitoring

Regular Call Monitoring and Review

Conduct weekly listening sessions focused on development rather than evaluation. Use real calls as teaching opportunities for the entire team.

Weekly Team Coaching Sessions

Create group learning opportunities where team members share best practices and learn from each other's successes and challenges.

Monthly Performance Evaluations

Track individual progress over time rather than just evaluating current performance. Focus on improvement trajectory and skill development.

Quarterly Training Updates

Keep training current with legal changes, market conditions, and system improvements. The business environment evolves constantly—training must evolve with it.

Performance Management and Development

Individual Coaching Plans

Develop personalized improvement strategies based on each team member's specific strengths and development needs. Not everyone requires the same type of support.

Team-Wide Best Practice Sharing

When someone achieves exceptional results, analyze what made it successful and share those insights with the entire team.

Recognition and Reward Systems

Celebrate excellence and improvement using specific, meaningful recognition that motivates continued growth and reinforces desired behaviors.

Continuous Improvement Initiatives

Encourage team members to contribute ideas for system improvements and process optimization. The people doing the work often have the best suggestions for enhancement.

Team Communication and Collaboration Systems

Daily Coordination Huddles

Brief daily meetings that address immediate challenges, share important updates, and maintain team cohesion and communication.

Weekly Training and Development Sessions

Regular skill building and problem-solving meetings that promote continuous learning and team development.

Monthly Performance and Planning Reviews

Individual and team progress assessment that provides feedback, sets goals, and maintains accountability for results.

Quarterly Strategic Planning and Goal Setting

Longer-term planning sessions that align individual development with firm growth objectives and market opportunities.

ADVANCED TEAM DEVELOPMENT STRATEGIES

Successful intake teams require ongoing development opportunities that prevent stagnation and promote retention of high-performing team members.

Career Advancement Pathways and Growth Opportunities

Senior Intake Specialist Roles

Create leadership positions that allow your best performers to take on training responsibilities and team coordination duties without leaving intake work entirely.

Specialization Development Opportunities

Allow team members to develop deep expertise in specific case types (DUI, felony, white-collar) or client segments that match their interests and strengths.

Management Track Development

Build future team leaders from your best performers by providing management training and gradual leadership responsibility increases.

Performance Optimization and Continuous Improvement

Individual Performance Coaching

Provide targeted skill development based on specific needs identified through systematic performance monitoring and analysis.

Peer Mentoring Programs

Pair experienced team members with newer staff to create ongoing support systems and knowledge transfer opportunities.

Innovation and Suggestion Programs

Create formal systems for team input on process improvements and new ideas that enhance effectiveness and efficiency.

Professional Development Investment

Invest in external training, certifications, and skill advancement opportunities that benefit both individual team members and firm capabilities.

TECHNOLOGY INTEGRATION AND SUPPORT SYSTEMS

Effective intake teams require seamless integration with technology systems that enhance rather than complicate their effectiveness.

Technology Training and Ongoing Support

CRM System Mastery

Ensure complete understanding and optimal utilization of customer relationship management functionality to support relationship building and follow-up effectiveness.

Communication Platform Integration

Train on seamless coordination across email, text messaging, and phone systems to provide consistent client experience across all touchpoints.

Performance Tracking and Reporting

Help team members understand their performance patterns and improvement opportunities through data analysis and self-assessment capabilities.

Process Integration and Workflow Optimization

Handoff Procedures and Coordination

Establish smooth transition protocols between team members and attorneys that ensure continuity and prevent important information from being lost.

Documentation Standards and Consistency

Implement uniform information capture and communication procedures that allow any team member to understand and continue any client interaction.

Quality Control Measures and Error Prevention

Build quality assurance into systems and processes rather than relying solely on after-the-fact error correction and performance evaluation.

Efficiency Improvement Without Quality Compromise

Streamline processes and eliminate unnecessary steps while maintaining the relationship building and trust development that drive conversion success.

CHAPTER SUMMARY

Training an effective intake team requires systematic hiring, structured onboarding, and ongoing development that maintains quality while building capacity for practice growth.

Hiring success depends on identifying candidates with high emotional intelligence, authentic caring, stress resilience, and coachability rather than just experience or technical knowledge.

The four-week onboarding process builds skills systematically while integrating new team members into firm culture and values that sustain long-term performance.

Maintaining consistency across multiple team members requires standardized frameworks that allow individual personality and communication style to emerge naturally.

Advanced development strategies including career advancement pathways, specialization opportunities, and continuous improvement initiatives retain high-performing team members while building organizational capability.

Technology integration and support systems enhance team effectiveness when properly implemented and maintained through ongoing training and optimization.

Investment in systematic team development creates competitive advantage that competitors cannot easily replicate, while ensuring that people facing criminal charges receive quality service during their most vulnerable moments.

When intake teams are properly hired, trained, and developed, they can maintain conversion rates while expanding capacity for practice growth and client service excellence.

In the final chapter, we'll explore the future of criminal defense intake through AI-powered optimization and implementation strategies that represent the cutting edge of practice development and client service enhancement.

CHAPTER 12:

AI-POWERED INTAKE OPTIMIZATION

The game-changing technology that most law firms aren't using effectively is artificial intelligence—specifically, AI-powered intake analysis and optimization. While your competitors are still guessing what works and what doesn't, AI provides objective, data-driven insights into every single intake conversation.

AI revolutionized intake quality at Ruane Attorneys in ways I never expected. For years, I thought I understood what made our best intake specialists successful. I was wrong about half of it. When we started using AI to analyze hundreds of intake calls, we discovered patterns that completely changed how we train, coach, and optimize performance.

For example, I believed empathy was mostly about tone of voice. AI showed us that empathy is actually measured by specific language patterns, response timing, and even the types of questions asked. I thought rapport building was subjective and couldn't be measured. AI proved that rapport follows predictable patterns that can be identified, taught, and replicated across team members.

This chapter will show you practical AI applications you can implement immediately for competitive advantage. You'll learn the proven 10-point AI grading system, how to use AI for real-time coaching, and how to set up automated content generation that personalizes every follow-up interaction.

THE TRANSFORMATION POTENTIAL OF AI IN INTAKE

Traditional intake coaching relies on subjective observations, limited sample sizes, and human bias in performance evaluation. Supervisors might listen to a few calls per month and provide general feedback based on their impressions and personal preferences.

AI changes everything by providing objective analysis of every conversation, identifying patterns across thousands of interactions, and delivering specific, actionable insights for improvement. This systematic approach transforms intake from an art into a science.

What AI Reveals That Human Analysis Misses

Micro-Patterns in Communication

AI can identify subtle patterns in successful conversations that human observers miss. For instance, AI might discover that prospects who receive empathy responses within 3 seconds of sharing emotional information are 40% more likely to hire you than those who experience longer response delays.

Language Pattern Correlations

AI analysis reveals which specific phrases, word choices, and communication patterns correlate with successful conversions. These insights allow you to train your team on exactly what language works rather than relying on general communication advice.

Predictive Indicators

AI can predict conversion probability based on early conversation indicators, allowing you to focus follow-up resources on the most promising prospects and adjust approach in real-time for struggling conversations.

The Competitive Advantage of Systematic Analysis

When you use AI to analyze hundreds or thousands of intake calls, you develop insights that competitors cannot replicate without similar data analysis. This creates sustainable competitive advantage based on systematic understanding rather than intuition.

THE COMPLETE 10-POINT AI GRADING SYSTEM

This comprehensive scoring system analyzes every intake call objectively across ten critical criteria, providing specific feedback for improvement and tracking progress over time.

Rapport Building Assessment (15 Points)

Empathy Markers and Connection Indicators

AI measures language warmth and emotional responsiveness by analyzing specific empathy phrases, response timing to emotional disclosures, and voice tone variations that indicate genuine concern.

The system looks for phrases like "That sounds really difficult" or "I can imagine how stressful this must be." It measures how long specialists pause after clients share emotional information—appropriate pauses indicate processing and empathy, while immediate responses suggest the specialist is waiting to talk rather than listening.

Voice Tone Analysis for Trust Building

AI detects subtle voice changes that indicate authentic empathy, such as slight pitch drops when showing concern—a natural human response most people don't realize they demonstrate.

Case Handling Confirmation (10 Points)

Firm Expertise Communication

AI detects whether specialists clearly communicated your firm's capability to handle specific case types and demonstrated confidence in your team's abilities.

Specialization Clarity

The system measures how effectively specialists position your firm's focused expertise rather than generic legal capability.

Empathy Display Analysis (15 Points)

Advanced Language Pattern Recognition

This sophisticated analysis includes validation phrase usage, emotional acknowledgment frequency, and client concern recognition with appropriate responses.

Emotional Intelligence Demonstration

AI tracks emotional intelligence throughout conversations by measuring response appropriateness to client emotional states and ability to maintain empathy under pressure.

Question Responsiveness Evaluation (15 Points)

Answer Completeness and Accuracy

AI tracks whether every client question receives thorough responses and identifies information gaps that damage trust and conversion probability.

Follow-Up Question Handling

The system measures curiosity demonstration and whether specialists explore client concerns thoroughly rather than providing surface-level responses.

Time Distribution Balance (10 Points)

Speaking Time Optimization

AI analyzes the ratio of client talk time versus specialist talk time, measuring strategic silence usage and conversation flow effectiveness.

Pace and Pause Assessment

The system identifies optimal conversation pacing that allows traumatized clients to process information without feeling rushed or overwhelmed.

Special Concerns Identification (10 Points)

Client-Specific Priority Recognition

AI recognizes whether specialists identify unique situation factors and address individual concerns rather than providing generic responses.

Personal Impact Factor Addressing

The system measures how effectively specialists acknowledge and respond to employment, family, and professional concerns that drive decision-making.

Financial Discussion Management (10 Points)

Value Communication Assessment

AI analyzes price presentation timing, value building before cost discussion, and payment option flexibility demonstration.

Investment Positioning

The system measures how effectively specialists position fees as investment in protection rather than cost of service.

Presumptive Language Avoidance (5 Points)

High-Pressure Tactic Detection

AI flags language patterns that assume hiring decisions or pressure prospects into commitments, measuring client autonomy respect and decision-making space provision.

Consultant vs. Salesperson Analysis

The system distinguishes between consultative guidance and aggressive sales tactics that destroy trust with traumatized clients.

Promises Made Management (5 Points)

Inappropriate Commitment Detection

AI flags unrealistic guarantees, inappropriate commitments, and ethical boundary violations that could create professional liability.

Professional Limitation Acknowledgment

The system measures appropriate transparency about case uncertainties and realistic expectation setting.

Knowledge Gaps Identification (5 Points)

Training Need Recognition

AI identifies areas where specialists need additional training or information to address client concerns effectively.

Continuous Learning Opportunities

The system highlights specific improvement areas and tracks progress over time for targeted development.

AI TRANSCRIPTION AND ANALYSIS IMPLEMENTATION

Recommended Platform Categories

Conversation Intelligence Tools

Platforms like Gong or Chorus, adapted for legal use, provide sophisticated analysis capabilities originally designed for sales teams but highly effective for intake optimization.

Legal-Specific Transcription Services

Services like Rev.com and Otter.ai with legal compliance features understand legal terminology and can handle attorney-client privilege concerns appropriately.

Custom AI Prompt Development

Instead of generic analysis, develop tailored prompts that analyze criminal defense intake conversations for specific psychological and conversion indicators relevant to your practice.

What AI Can Identify and Measure

Emotional Tone and Stress Indicators

AI detects when clients become more or less stressed during conversations and whether specialists respond appropriately to emotional changes.

Speaking Pace and Pause Pattern Analysis

The system identifies conversation flow optimization opportunities and determines when specialists talk too fast for traumatized clients to process information.

Interruption Frequency and Timing

AI measures active listening demonstration by tracking interruption patterns—effective specialists rarely interrupt clients sharing their experiences.

Question-to-Statement Ratio

The system distinguishes between consultative approaches (more questions) and lecture-style approaches (more statements) that reduce engagement.

Outcome Prediction Capabilities

AI can predict conversion probability with high accuracy based on conversation patterns identified in the first ten minutes of calls.

AI-POWERED TRAINING AND COACHING SYSTEMS

Personalized Training Program Development

Individual Strength and Weakness Identification

AI provides completely objective skill assessment that eliminates guesswork about team member development needs.

Customized Coaching Recommendations

The system generates specific improvement strategies for each team member—one person might need empathy language development while another requires follow-up questioning improvement.

Progress Tracking and Development Monitoring

AI provides objective measurement of improvement over time, allowing you to track skill development quantitatively rather than subjectively.

Real-Time Coaching Applications

Live Call Coaching Integration

Advanced systems provide real-time prompts during calls: "Client mentioned job concerns—address professional licensing impact" or "Client stress level increasing—slow down and provide reassurance."

Immediate Quality Assessment

AI delivers real-time scoring and improvement recommendations while conversations are happening, allowing for immediate course correction.

Suggested Response and Technique Prompts

The system recommends phrases and approaches based on what works best in similar situations, providing just-in-time coaching support.

Red Flag Warning Systems

AI alerts supervisors to difficult situations requiring immediate intervention or additional support for struggling specialists.

Advanced Coaching Integration Features

AI-Generated Role-Play Scenarios

The system creates practice situations based on real call patterns from your actual clients, providing relevant training opportunities.

Skill Gap Analysis and Focused Training

AI identifies specific weakness areas and generates targeted exercises designed to address individual development needs.

Success Pattern Replication

The system identifies what top performers do differently and teaches those techniques across the entire team systematically.

AI CONTENT GENERATION FOR OPTIMIZATION

Follow-Up Email Automation and Personalization

Custom Content Based on Client Concerns

AI generates personalized follow-up emails addressing specific concerns mentioned during intake calls. Employment worries trigger career protection content, while family concerns generate family security messaging.

Demographic and Case-Specific Messaging

First-time DUI clients receive different content than repeat offenders, and professional clients get different messaging than blue-collar workers.

Optimal Timing and Sequence Recommendations

AI determines the best send times and frequency based on when specific client types are most likely to engage with follow-up communications.

Script Development and Continuous Optimization

Highest-Converting Language Pattern Analysis

AI identifies the most effective language patterns from successful calls and incorporates them into script development and training materials.

Performance-Driven Refinement

Scripts improve continuously based on performance data rather than subjective preferences or assumptions about what should work.

Client Type Customization

AI develops specialized approaches for different client characteristics that can be implemented in real-time during conversations.

Content Performance Analytics

Engagement and Conversion Tracking

Every piece of AI-generated content is tracked for effectiveness, allowing continuous optimization based on actual results rather than assumptions.

A/B Testing Integration

AI automatically tests different messaging approaches and optimizes content based on performance comparisons.

ROI Measurement and Value Demonstration

The system tracks direct correlation between AI-generated content and successful retainer agreements, proving the value of technology investment.

IMPLEMENTATION STRATEGY AND ROADMAP

Technology Requirements and Investment

Hardware and Software Specifications

Adequate computer processing power, internet bandwidth, and storage capacity for handling large amounts of call data and analysis.

Monthly Subscription Costs

Budget planning for AI tools and platforms typically ranges from $200-500 per month for comprehensive systems, depending on call volume and feature requirements.

Integration Complexity Assessment

Most systems can be fully operational within 2-4 weeks with proper planning and technical support.

Staff Training and Adoption Strategy

Change Management and Resistance Handling

Address team concerns about AI monitoring by positioning it as coaching and development tool rather than surveillance system.

Training Timeline and Milestones

Plan for 2-3 weeks of adjustment period with ongoing support and gradually increasing independence with AI tools.

Performance Incentive Integration

Motivate team adoption through AI-driven bonuses and recognition that reward improvement and excellence.

Privacy, Legal, and Ethical Considerations

Legal Compliance Requirements

Ensure proper call recording consent and disclosure, secure data storage protocols, and appropriate privacy protection for client information.

Professional Liability and Risk Management

Consider insurance implications and implement risk mitigation strategies for technology-enhanced practice management.

Ethical Implementation Guidelines

Maintain appropriate client notification about AI usage without creating concern, balance performance monitoring with privacy respect, and establish data usage and retention policies.

FOUR-PHASE IMPLEMENTATION ROADMAP

Phase 1 (Month 1): Foundation and Basic Setup

Technology selection and procurement, basic system installation and configuration, team introduction and initial training, pilot program with limited scope and evaluation.

Phase 2 (Month 2): Full Implementation and Training

Complete system deployment, comprehensive staff training program, performance baseline establishment, and process refinement based on initial results.

Phase 3 (Month 3): Advanced Features and Optimization

Advanced analytics and reporting implementation, custom AI prompt development, integration with marketing and follow-up systems, performance-based incentive integration.

Phase 4 (Month 4+): Continuous Improvement and Innovation

Ongoing system optimization, advanced feature adoption, team excellence development, ROI analysis and strategic planning for future enhancements.

MEASURING SUCCESS AND ROI

Performance Improvement Metrics

Track conversion rate improvements, client satisfaction enhancements, team development acceleration, and efficiency gains from AI implementation.

Competitive Advantage Development

AI-optimized systems create sustainable competitive advantage that competitors cannot easily replicate without similar data analysis and technology investment.

Long-Term Value Creation

Technology adoption now positions your practice for continued advantage as AI capabilities expand and become more sophisticated over time.

CHAPTER SUMMARY

AI-powered intake optimization transforms subjective performance assessment into objective, data-driven improvement through systematic analysis of every client interaction.

The 10-point AI grading system provides comprehensive evaluation across all critical intake skills, enabling targeted training and measurable improvement over time.

AI transcription and analysis tools reveal communication patterns and success indicators that human observation cannot detect reliably or consistently.

Real-time coaching applications and personalized training programs accelerate team development while maintaining consistency across multiple staff members.

Automated content generation and optimization create personalized client experiences that improve conversion rates and follow-up effectiveness.

Systematic implementation through a four-phase roadmap ensures successful adoption while maintaining legal compliance and ethical standards.

The competitive advantage created through AI adoption compounds over time, creating sustainable differentiation in increasingly competitive markets.

Criminal defense firms that implement AI-powered intake optimization now will have significant advantages over those who wait, as the technology becomes more sophisticated and data insights become more valuable with extended use.

This represents the future of criminal defense intake—systematic, measurable, and continuously improving through technology that enhances rather than replaces human connection and empathy.

CONCLUSION: BUILDING A PRACTICE THAT SERVES JUSTICE

You now have a complete system for criminal defense intake and sales mastery that combines psychological understanding, systematic methodology, and cutting-edge technology. From understanding client trauma responses to implementing AI-powered optimization, these techniques work together to ensure that people facing criminal charges receive quality representation while building sustainable practice growth.

The ultimate goal transcends business development—it's about serving justice by connecting skilled attorneys with clients who need their expertise during the most challenging times of their lives. When you master these systems, you create a practice that grows while making a meaningful difference in your community.

Implementation of these techniques requires commitment, systematic approach, and ongoing refinement. But the results—higher conversion rates, better client satisfaction, sustainable growth, and meaningful contribution to justice—justify the investment in mastering criminal defense intake and sales.

The people who call you need your help. Your practice needs systematic growth. The justice system needs attorneys who can effectively advocate for their services. This comprehensive system serves all those goals while building the kind of practice that makes a lasting difference in people's lives.

OFFICIAL AI PROMPT FOR GRADING CALLS

Use 10-point intake scoring rubric with a grading matrix, score out of 100, detailed justification, and improvement notes.

Analyze the following transcript of an intake call between an intake specialist and a caller. Evaluate the call based on the objectives below, and provide a detailed report with a numerical score out of 100, reflecting the intake specialist's performance. Additionally, include a grading matrix to show how each section impacts the final score.

Objectives and Scoring Criteria (Total: 100%)

1. Rapport Building – 15%
  - Objective: Assess whether the intake specialist builds rapport with the caller using warm, empathetic language that establishes trust.
  - Scoring: Full points if the specialist consistently uses empathetic statements and engages the caller in a friendly

manner. Partial points if rapport is attempted but lacks consistency or depth.

2. Case Handling Confirmation – 10%
- Objective: Determine if the intake specialist clearly confirms whether the firm can handle the caller's case type.
- Scoring: Full points for a clear statement on the firm's capability to manage the case and next steps if relevant. Partial points if the response is unclear or lacks detail.

3. Empathy Display – 15%
- Objective: Evaluate whether the intake specialist acknowledges the caller's emotions with empathetic statements.
- Scoring: Full points for consistently recognizing the caller's emotions and concerns. Partial points if empathy is shown but lacks consistency.

4. Question Responsiveness – 15%
- Objective: Analyze if the intake specialist adequately addresses all questions posed by the caller.
- Scoring: Full points if all questions are answered clearly and thoroughly. Partial points if some questions are missed or only partially addressed.

5. Time Distribution Balance – 10%
- Objective: Ensure the intake specialist balances speaking time to allow the caller to explain their situation fully.
- Scoring: Full points if time distribution is balanced between the intake specialist and caller. Partial points if the intake specialist speaks disproportionately.

6. Identification of Special Concerns – 10%

- Objective: Identify if the intake specialist listens for, acknowledges, and addresses specific concerns or unique needs (e.g., urgency, privacy, employment impact).
- Scoring: Full points for recognizing and addressing caller-specific concerns. Partial points if concerns are acknowledged but inadequately addressed.

7. Financial Discussion and Payment Responsibility – 10%
- Objective: Determine if the intake specialist discusses potential costs and identifies the responsible party for payment.
- Scoring: Full points if financial aspects and payment responsibilities are addressed clearly. Partial points if finances are mentioned but lack clarity or completeness.

8. Presumptive Language Usage – 5%
- Objective: Assess whether the intake specialist uses presumptive language, confirming that the client is calling to hire an attorney and ready to take next steps - Scoring: Full points if language remains presumptive of the close. Partial points if the specialist uses language that doesn't obtain caller commitment.

9. Promises Made to Caller – 5%
- Objective: Identify any guarantees or promises made to the caller regarding outcomes, actions, or timelines.
- Scoring: Full points if promises are avoided or qualified. Partial points if any implied guarantees are made without proper disclaimers.

10. Knowledge and Training Gaps – 5%
- Objective: Note questions the intake specialist cannot answer, indicating areas where additional training may be beneficial.
- Scoring: Full points if the intake specialist confidently answers all questions without noticeable knowledge gaps. Partial points if there are any training gaps identified.

Report Format

1. Provide an overall score out of 100, with each section scored based on the criteria above.
2. Include a grading matrix showing each section's weight, score, and impact on the total grade, with a final score summary.
3. Highlight specific examples from the transcript to justify each score, and note areas for improvement where applicable.

Final Score Calculation: Sum the totals to generate a score out of 100. Provide a summary explaining the final score and areas for improvement.

CHAPTER 13:

STAY TOP-OF-MIND FOLLOW-UP SYSTEMS

There's a critical difference between following up for sales and staying connected for relationships. Most attorneys completely miss this distinction, and it's costing them millions in referral revenue over the course of their careers.

Traditional attorney follow-up looks predictably inadequate: six months of silence after case resolution, followed by a desperate newsletter that screams "PLEASE REFER US CASES!" followed by more silence. Then attorneys wonder why past clients never refer anyone despite being satisfied with their representation.

The fundamental problem with most attorney follow-up is that it's entirely focused on what the attorney wants rather than what the client needs. It's transactional when it should be relational. It treats past clients like a database to be mined rather than relationships to be nurtured.

This chapter will show you psychology-based long-term client relationship systems that generate consistent referrals year after year. You'll learn why clients forget their criminal defense attorneys, how to position yourself as a helpful expert rather than just a vendor, and how to build relationships that compound over time into sustainable referral generation.

This isn't about sending more follow-up emails. This is about becoming the attorney people naturally think of when legal issues arise in their circle of influence.

THE PSYCHOLOGY OF "TOP OF MIND" FOR LEGAL SERVICES

Understanding why clients forget their attorneys is crucial for developing effective long-term relationship strategies. The psychology of criminal defense creates unique challenges that most attorneys don't address systematically.

Why Clients Forget Their Criminal Defense Attorneys

Crisis Resolution Mentality

Once their case resolves, clients instinctively want to forget the entire traumatic experience. They associate you with one of the worst periods of their life, not necessarily with the solution you provided. This psychological distance is natural but destructive for long-term relationship building.

Life Compartmentalization

Most people view legal issues as completely separate from their normal daily life. They put that entire experience in a mental compartment and try never to open it again. Unfortunately, this compartmentalization includes you and your firm.

Negative Association Avoidance

Criminal charges create trauma memories that people actively avoid revisiting. While you solved their problem, you can become part of the negative memory they prefer to suppress rather than a positive resource they want to remember.

Professional Distance Maintenance

The formal attorney-client relationship often doesn't feel personal to clients. You solved their problem professionally and competently, but you weren't their friend or trusted advisor beyond the specific legal issue.

The Referral Psychology and Client Mindset

Trust Transfer Mechanism

People refer professionals they trust personally, not just those who performed competent work. There must be a personal connection that extends beyond professional competence. Technical skill gets you hired; personal trust gets you referred.

Relationship Strength Impact

Strong personal relationships generate referrals consistently; transactional relationships don't. If clients feel like they hired a service, they won't think to refer you. If they feel like they have an ongoing relationship with you, referrals become natural.

Timing and Availability Awareness

Potential referrers need current knowledge of your practice and availability. They need to know you're still in business, still taking cases, and still providing excellent service. Without ongoing contact, they assume you might not be available or interested.

Positive Association Requirement

Clients must feel genuinely positive about their entire experience before referring others. If thinking about you brings up negative memories or mixed feelings, they won't risk their reputation by making referrals.

The "Helpful Expert" Positioning Strategy

Traditional Approach Limitations

Most attorneys position themselves as: "Call us if you get arrested again or need legal help." This approach is limited because it assumes future legal problems and maintains the crisis-focused relationship.

Relationship-Building Approach

Better positioning: "We're your ongoing resource for understanding legal issues affecting your life." This positions you as a helpful advisor rather than just an emergency contact.

Mindset Transformation

Shift from being their "criminal defense attorney" to being their "legal resource and advisor." This subtle but important distinction changes how they think about you and when they consider contacting you.

LONG-TERM RELATIONSHIP BUILDING VS. SALES-FOCUSED FOLLOW-UP

Understanding the differences between relationship building and sales follow-up is crucial for developing effective long-term client communication strategies.

Common Problems with Traditional Attorney Follow-Up

Overly Sales-Focused Approach

Traditional follow-up constantly asks for business, referrals, or new cases. Every communication has an obvious agenda that benefits the attorney rather than the client. This approach feels manipulative and damages relationship development.

Impersonal Mass Communication

Generic newsletters and automated messages without personalization feel obviously mass-produced. Clients can immediately tell it's bulk communication, and bulk communication doesn't build personal relationships.

Infrequent and Sporadic Contact

Many attorneys maintain complete silence for months, then suddenly reach out when they want something. This pattern signals that the relationship only matters when the attorney needs business.

Irrelevant Content Delivery

Legal updates that have nothing to do with clients' daily lives feel like attorney-focused content rather than client-focused value. Generic legal news doesn't demonstrate understanding of their specific needs or interests.

Relationship-Building Communication Philosophy

Value-First Communication Strategy

Every communication should provide genuine value that improves clients' lives or understanding, regardless of whether it generates immediate business for your firm.

Daily Life Legal Updates

Share changes in laws that affect everyday activities and rights: "New Connecticut law affects your rights during traffic stops" is relevant to everyone and positions you as a helpful resource.

Community News and Involvement

Demonstrate firm participation in local events and charitable activities. Show clients you're part of their community, not just a business operating within it.

Educational Content About Rights

Develop "Know Your Rights" series and practical legal guidance that helps clients feel more confident and informed in legal situations they might encounter.

Personal Milestone Sharing

Share firm achievements, attorney recognition, and professional growth in ways that allow clients to feel proud of "their" attorney's success.

Personal Connection Maintenance Techniques

Birthday and Holiday Greetings

Remember important personal dates and celebrations, but make communications genuinely personal rather than obviously automated mass messages.

Case Resolution Anniversary Recognition

Acknowledge successful outcome anniversaries with positive framing: "It's been two years since we resolved your case. Hope life has been treating you well!"

Life Event Acknowledgments

Recognize new jobs, marriages, children, home purchases, and other significant life events. Show genuine interest in their lives beyond their legal cases.

Community Involvement Invitations

Create opportunities for face-to-face relationship building through educational seminars, charity events, and social gatherings that bring clients together.

Professional Resource Positioning

Open "Ask the Attorney" Policy

Maintain a standing invitation for quick legal questions that positions you as their go-to resource for legal guidance, even on matters outside your practice area.

Quick Legal Guidance Provision

Provide brief answers to simple legal concerns through five-minute phone calls that build lifetime loyalty and demonstrate ongoing accessibility.

Referrals to Other Professionals

Connect clients with accountants, real estate agents, financial planners, and other professionals. Become the person who knows people and can make valuable introductions.

General Legal Education and Awareness

Provide ongoing education about legal rights and responsibilities that affect daily life, positioning yourself as a trusted source of legal information.

SPECIFIC SYSTEMS AND IMPLEMENTATION TACTICS

Effective long-term relationship building requires systematic approaches that combine personal touches with scalable communication strategies.

The "Legal Life" Newsletter System Framework

Monthly Educational Theme Calendar

Develop consistent monthly themes that provide relevant value throughout the year:

January: New laws and regulations affecting daily life
February: Family legal issues and relationship rights
March: Spring cleaning legal checklist and document updates
April: Tax season legal implications and IRS interaction rights
May: Travel and vacation legal tips and emergency procedures
June: Summer activity legal awareness and safety considerations
July: Independence Day celebration of rights and civic responsibilities
August: Back-to-school legal issues and parent rights
September: Fall legal preparation and annual review reminders

October: Halloween safety and holiday legal considerations
November: Thanksgiving gratitude message and firm appreciation
December: Year-end legal review and holiday wishes

The "Three Touch" Quarterly Relationship System

Touch 1 - Educational Value

Provide legal information directly relevant to their current life situation based on what you know about their circumstances and interests.

Touch 2 - Personal Connection

Acknowledge birthdays, anniversaries, or milestone celebrations that demonstrate you remember them as individuals rather than just former clients.

Touch 3 - Resource Provision

Introduce them to other professionals or valuable services they might need, positioning yourself as a connector and resource hub.

The "Anniversary Approach" for Case Resolution Recognition

Develop sincere, personal communication for case resolution anniversaries:

"Hi John, I was just thinking about you as we approached the anniversary of resolving your case. I hope this past year has brought you everything you hoped for when we first talked about your situation.

I wanted you to know that if any legal questions come up in your life—big or small—please don't hesitate to reach out. I'm always happy to point you in the right direction, even if it's not something I handle directly.

Hope you and your family are doing wonderfully!

Best regards, Jay"

Notice the tone: it's personal, helpful, and contains no sales pitch or request for business.

Technology Integration and Automation

CRM System Automation Capabilities

Implement birthday and anniversary tracking with automatic reminders, communication history logging, referral source tracking, and engagement level monitoring.

Email Marketing Platform Integration

Develop segmented lists by client categories, automated sequences for different client types, personal touch point scheduling, and response tracking with engagement analysis.

The "Concentric Circles" Client Relationship Approach

Inner Circle (A+ Clients and Active Referrers)

Quarterly personal touches plus monthly valuable communications. These are your most important relationship investments.

Middle Circle (Good Clients and Potential Referrers)

Bi-annual personal touches plus monthly educational communications. Maintain awareness without overwhelming.

Outer Circle (All Past Clients)

Annual personal touches plus monthly educational communications. Stay connected without major time investment.

ADVANCED RELATIONSHIP STRATEGIES

Sophisticated relationship building goes beyond communication to create genuine value and community connections.

The "Resource Hub" Community Positioning

Professional Network Maintenance

Develop and maintain relationships with accountants, real estate agents, financial planners, and other professionals who serve your clients' broader needs.

"Person Who Knows People" Reputation

Become the go-to connector in your professional community. When clients need any professional service, they should think of calling you first for recommendations.

Value-Added Connections and Introductions

Provide networking opportunities as a client service that extends your value far beyond legal representation.

The "Educational Authority" Establishment

Client Educational Seminar Hosting

Host regular workshops on legal topics affecting daily life that position you as the community legal education resource.

Exclusive Client-Only Content Development

Create special access materials and information that make past clients feel like VIP members of your professional community.

Thought Leadership in Client Community

Work to be recognized as the legal expert in their social and professional circles through consistent, valuable content and community involvement.

90-DAY IMPLEMENTATION PLAN

Month 1: System Setup and Foundation

Technology selection and integration, initial content development, communication template creation, and team training on relationship building principles.

Month 2: Content Creation and Process Development

Newsletter template development, personal touch point systems, automation setup, and testing with select client groups.

Month 3: Full System Launch and Monitoring

Complete implementation across all client segments, engagement monitoring and analysis, performance measurement, and system refinement based on initial results.

Success Metrics and Measurement

Email Open and Click Rates

Track engagement levels and content effectiveness to optimize communication strategies.

Referral Generation from Past Clients

Monitor relationship strength and trust indicators through actual referral activity.

Client Response and Engagement Levels

Measure active participation and communication quality to assess relationship development.

Revenue from Repeat and Referral Business

Calculate financial impact of relationship investment to justify continued resource allocation.

CHAPTER SUMMARY

Long-term client relationship building requires understanding the psychology of why clients forget their criminal defense attorneys and developing systematic approaches to maintain positive, valuable connections over time.

The shift from sales-focused follow-up to relationship-building communication creates genuine value for clients while positioning attorneys as helpful resources rather than just emergency contacts.

Systematic approaches including monthly newsletters, quarterly personal touches, and anniversary recognition maintain consistent contact without feeling intrusive or sales-focused.

Technology integration enables scalable relationship building while maintaining personal touches that differentiate your firm from competitors who rely solely on automated communications.

Advanced strategies including community positioning, educational authority establishment, and professional network development create compound relationship value that generates referrals consistently over time.

The investment in long-term relationship building pays dividends for decades through referral generation, repeat business, and community reputation that cannot be replicated through marketing alone.

When clients think of you as a helpful resource and trusted advisor rather than just their former attorney, they naturally refer others and maintain loyalty that sustains practice growth through relationship rather than constant new client acquisition.

This systematic approach to client relationship management transforms one-time transactions into lifetime professional relationships that benefit both the practice and the community it serves.

CONCLUSION:

THE TRANSFORMATION FRAMEWORK AND YOUR NEXT STEPS

We've covered substantial ground together in this comprehensive guide to criminal defense intake and sales mastery. From understanding the psychology of clients in crisis to implementing AI-powered optimization systems, you now have a complete framework for transforming your practice through superior intake performance.

But having knowledge isn't enough. Implementation is everything. And implementation is where most attorneys struggle, not because of lack of ability, but because sustainable change requires ongoing support, accountability, and systematic application of proven principles.

THE COMPLETE TRANSFORMATION FRAMEWORK

Throughout these thirteen chapters, we've built a systematic approach to criminal defense intake that addresses every aspect of client conversion and relationship building:

Foundation Psychology (Chapters 1-3)

You learned why criminal clients think and behave differently from normal consumers, how trauma affects decision-making processes, and why traditional sales approaches fail catastrophically with people experiencing crisis situations.

Understanding client psychology is the foundation that makes everything else work. Without this knowledge, even the best techniques feel manipulative and produce inconsistent results.

The B.U.I.L.D. System and Core Methodology (Chapters 4-7)

You mastered the systematic approach that converts prospects into clients through trust building rather than pressure tactics. You learned how to handle the three major objections that kill most criminal defense conversions, how to position value effectively, and how to close consultatively while respecting client autonomy.

These systematic approaches ensure consistency regardless of personality type, experience level, or market conditions. When you have proven frameworks, you don't need to be brilliant on every call—you just need to be systematic.

Advanced Implementation Strategies (Chapters 8-12)

You discovered how to measure and improve performance through data-driven analysis, how to build and train effective teams while maintaining legal compliance, and how cutting-edge AI technology can optimize every aspect of your intake process for predictable improvement.

These advanced strategies separate exceptional practices from merely competent ones. They create competitive advantages that compound over time and become increasingly difficult for competitors to replicate.

Long-Term Relationship Building (Chapter 13)

You learned how to transform past clients into referral sources through value-first communication and helpful expert positioning that generates business for decades.

This final piece transforms your practice from constantly needing new client acquisition to building sustainable growth through relationships and reputation.

THE TRANSFORMATION YOU CAN ACHIEVE

This comprehensive system represents the exact framework that has built multiple successful criminal defense practices. When implemented systematically, these strategies create predictable improvements across every aspect of your business:

Conversion Rate Enhancement

Your ability to convert prospects into clients improves predictably rather than randomly. You understand exactly why some conversations succeed while others fail, and you can systematically address weakness areas.

Team Development Acceleration

Systematic training approaches and AI-powered coaching accelerate skill development across your entire team. New staff members become effective faster, and experienced team members continue improving rather than plateauing.

Scalable Quality Growth

Proper delegation frameworks and team building systems allow you to grow capacity without sacrificing conversion effectiveness or client satisfaction.

Sustainable Competitive Advantage

Advanced systems and technology implementation create advantages that compound over time and become increasingly difficult for competitors to replicate without similar systematic development.

Long-Term Referral Generation

Relationship building systems turn past clients into advocates who generate business consistently without ongoing marketing investment.

THE IMPLEMENTATION CHALLENGE

Understanding why most attorneys struggle with implementation helps you avoid common pitfalls and create accountability for your own development:

Information Overload Without Prioritization

Having comprehensive strategies without clear next steps creates paralysis rather than progress. Knowing what to do isn't useful without understanding where to start and what sequence to follow.

Lack of Accountability and External Support

Solo implementation often fails because there's no external pressure or encouragement to follow through when daily practice demands compete for attention and energy.

Analysis Paralysis from Perfectionism

Waiting for perfect systems instead of starting with good approaches and improving over time prevents progress. Excellence develops through iteration, not initial perfection.

Competing Priorities and Time Management

Practice demands make it difficult to focus on business development and system building without external accountability and structured implementation support.

THE REALITY OF SUSTAINABLE CHANGE

Most attorneys consume training content, get motivated, start implementing, hit challenges, and gradually drift back to previous methods. Six months later, nothing has fundamentally changed except they have more unused knowledge.

This pattern isn't a character flaw—it's human nature. Sustainable change requires:

Ongoing Support and Guidance

Complex systems require ongoing refinement based on real-world application and changing market conditions.

Peer Community for Problem-Solving

When implementation challenges arise, learning from others who've faced similar issues accelerates progress and prevents abandonment of proven strategies.

Accountability for Consistent Application

External accountability creates motivation to continue implementation when internal motivation wavers during difficult periods.

Continuous Learning and Adaptation

Markets, technology, and client expectations evolve constantly. Successful implementation requires ongoing education and system refinement.

YOUR IMPLEMENTATION OPTIONS

You have several paths forward for implementing these strategies:

Solo Implementation

Apply these techniques independently using the frameworks and templates provided throughout this guide. This approach requires strong self-discipline and systematic application but can be effective for highly motivated attorneys.

Community-Based Implementation

Join communities of criminal defense attorneys facing similar challenges and working toward similar goals. Peer support and shared problem-solving accelerate implementation and prevent common pitfalls.

Systematic Coaching and Support

Invest in ongoing coaching and support that provides accountability, customized guidance, and systematic implementation planning based on your specific practice needs and market conditions.

THE CHOICE AHEAD

You have comprehensive knowledge and proven systems. The difference between attorneys who transform their practices and those who remain frustrated with their current results lies entirely in implementation consistency and quality.

Consider these questions as you decide your next steps:

Are you satisfied with your current conversion rates and growth trajectory, or do you want predictable improvement?

Do you prefer working in isolation with implementation challenges, or would community support and accountability accelerate your progress?

Are you willing to invest time and resources in systematic improvement, or do you prefer maintaining current approaches?

Do you want criminal defense-specific strategies and support, or are generic business development approaches sufficient for your needs?

THE COMPOUND EFFECT OF SYSTEMATIC IMPROVEMENT

Small, consistent improvements in intake performance create dramatic long-term results through compound growth. A 10% improvement in conversion rates doesn't just increase revenue by 10%—it increases referrals, client satisfaction, team confidence, and market reputation in ways that multiply the initial improvement.

When you systematically implement these strategies with proper support and accountability, you create sustainable competitive advantages that benefit your practice for decades while serving justice by ensuring people get quality representation during their most vulnerable moments.

YOUR NEXT ACTION

Knowledge without implementation serves no one. The people who call your practice need skilled representation during one of the most difficult periods of their lives. Your practice needs systematic growth to achieve its potential. The justice system needs attorneys who can effectively advocate for their services.

Choose your implementation path based on your commitment level, available resources, and desired timeline for results. Whether you proceed independently or with community support, the most important decision is to begin systematic application of these proven principles immediately.

Your practice transformation starts with your next action. The knowledge is complete. The systems are proven. The only remaining variable is your commitment to consistent implementation.

The attorneys who master these systems don't just build more successful practices—they ensure that people facing criminal charges receive the quality representation they deserve while building sustainable businesses that serve their communities for decades.

Your clients need you to be as effective as possible at converting qualified prospects into retained clients. This comprehensive system provides everything necessary to achieve that goal.

The transformation begins now.

ABOUT THE AUTHOR

Jay Ruane is the founder and CEO of Ruane Attorneys at Law, a criminal defense firm that has grown from a solo practice to a multi-million-dollar operation serving clients throughout Connecticut. Since 1998, Jay has represented thousands of clients facing criminal charges while developing systematic approaches to practice management and client acquisition that have transformed his firm into one of the most successful criminal defense practices in the state.

Recognizing that most attorneys struggle with the business side of law practice, Jay founded The Criminal Mastermind in 2023 — the only coaching community focused exclusively on criminal defense attorneys. Through this platform, he teaches practice management, marketing strategies, and systematic client conversion techniques to criminal defense lawyers across the nation.

Jay is a frequent speaker at criminal defense conferences and contributes regularly to The Champion, the magazine of the National Association of Criminal Defense Lawyers, where he writes about firm management and business development.

A graduate of law school with nearly three decades of criminal defense experience, Jay has been recognized by his peers for both his legal advocacy and his leadership in advancing the criminal defense bar. He is admitted to practice in Connecticut and New York and the United States Supreme Court..

Jay lives in Connecticut with his wife Jill and their four children. When not working with clients or coaching attorneys, he enjoys golf, learning guitar, and supporting local charities focused on justice and community development.

For more information about Jay's work with criminal defense attorneys, visit thecriminalmastermind.com.

www.ingramcontent.com/pod-product-compliance
Lightning Source LLC
Chambersburg PA
CBHW070308200326
41518CB00010B/1930